WHITE MAGIC

TITANIA'S BOOK OF FAVORITE SPELLS

WHITE MAGIC

TITANIA'S BOOK OF FAVORITE SPELLS

TITANIA HARDIE

PHOTOGRAPHS BY SARA MORRIS

CEDCO PUBLISHING

DIFFUSIVE: FOR THE GROWING GOOD

PARTLY DEPENDENT ON UNHISTORIC

HINGS ARE NOT SO ILL WITH YOU AND

T HAVE BEEN, IS HALF OWING TO THE

ED FAITHFULLY A HIDDEN LIFE, AND

TOMBS."

the finale of Middlemarch

Introducing the art of magic ★

To accept that potions, brews, or chanted rhymes can alter our circumstances may invite us to return to the days of reading fairy tales, expecting that everything can turn out well in the end if you believe it can. Some adults dismiss this belief as foolish and irrational; we have learned that money doesn't grow on trees, that it is nearly impossible to find the end of a rainbow—never mind the pot of gold, and that kissing any number of frogs is unlikely to yield anything more than a wart on the lip. None of this, however, appears to diminish our belief in the mystery of life. ★ Webster's Dictionary defines magic as "... the use of ceremonies, charms, and spells ... to produce or prevent a particular result"; so perhaps there is really nothing extraordinary about it. It works on the simple premise that by harnessing the strength of one's thinking, the force of the "wish-power," and marrying that to the clever use and deft handling of herbs (which have complex chemical properties), we can change the way we are perceived by others, improve our health, and boost our confidence, all with lasting and beneficial effect. ★ The marriage of spirit and psyche has a long history in the treatment of illness. Until the seventeenth century, doctors recognized that physical healing of our body would be truly effective only if the spirit were also healed. The instructions given to gather herbs at certain specific times of day or night—which are now thought genuinely to increase the herb's potency—always promised a cure if God's will was also invoked; faith was a prerequisite of healing. Now, so many centuries later, we are returning to the understanding that mind, body, and spirit are indivisibly interwoven. ★ With this in mind, I invite you to test the efficacy of magic with the help of the spells that follow. There is no need to become an apprentice witch or espouse the whole pagan philosophy, but three rules for working the magic should be adhered to. Choose a spell that is suitable (there's no point burning candles to ignite a passionate affair if your loved one is miles away from you); perform your spell at a good, relaxed time (you'll never succeed if your mind is skipping ahead to writing your shopping list or remembering to feed the neighbor's cat); and, most importantly perhaps, never do a spell that attempts to harm someone (you've heard it said, and it is absolutely true, that it will bounce back on you with greater force). ★ Exercise caution with magic. The ingredients you use may come from the garden and the pantry, but magic is nevertheless a powerful tool. You have a moral obligation not to try to use it to gain control over, or hurt, someone else. Use it instead as your own secret weapon—like wearing a sexy bra or a fabulous designer fragrance. Expertise in magic endowed Merlin with a charisma more tangible perhaps than that of his king. If performing your spell helps you feel you've taken more control of your life, and therefore better about yourself, you've won half the battle.

The witch's tools ★ The stuff of making spells is perfectly accessible to anyone.

It might seem disappointing to admit that most of the ingredients you will need can be purchased at a good supermarket, but there is really no need to make difficulties where there are none. ★ Many people feel their magic is imbued with greater strength and mystery if certain ingredients are "gathered by moonlight", or require a trip to a specialist supplier of herbs or oils. If this works for you, then you should continue, making a treasure hunt for the items needed for a spell. Certainly, it helps to create a good level of concentration and mood for performing magic if there has been a sense of ceremony in the collection of the items. ★ Spellmaking is powerful, though, whether the ingredients have come from a local grocery store or by mail order—as long as your attitude is right. Most of the objects used in spells are ordinary—it is what you do with them and how you "charm" them that turns an ordinary dinner candle into a magic wand, or a fondue pot into a cauldron. ★ If your mind is strong and your heart pure, your magic-making will have an excellent chance of succeeding without too much preliminary ritual; but if you want to be sure of giving your spells their best chance of working, take time to get the right tools together and to understand the psychological concept of working magic. Any effort you spend in creating the right mood, preparing the area you'll work in, and learning how to work with the tides of the moon is effort well spent. It is also wise to collect a few useful items that you will need on a regular basis. ★ A clever witch's supermarket cart will make straight for the supplies of fresh herbs. Always buy herbs if they're there, and dry them yourself if need be. Garlic and basil are used over and over in magic—with the added advantage that they can be whisked up into a pesto sauce if you're landed with unexpected dinner guests. If your windowsill permits and you can grow fresh herbs, all to the good. ★ Candles of any color will never go to waste in a witchy household. Used repeatedly in spells for love, health, luck, and money, they will also come in handy in an electricity blackout. Whenever possible, buy scented candles, which have uses in healing and setting the atmosphere for all magic workings. ★ Pop into the next aisle and find the honey—an absolute must-have for spells. Choose the one you prefer on toast, but if you can find an exotic blend (such as clover or lavender honey), so much the better. ★ In the wine section, choose whatever your budget and willpower (hard to leave a bottle of champagne until you want it for a love potion) will allow. Bubbles have the most value to a witch, but any strong wine can form the basis of your brew. ★ One of the most important tools you will need is a red cord or ribbon—more helpful than a crystal ball for putting you in touch with the spirits. This is used again and again for thought transference and contacting people. It is important to use good-quality ribbon, so a visit to the notions department is recommended here — gift-wrap ribbons have entirely the wrong feel. Buy several yards, but cut a special length of one yard, which will become your personal message line. ★ CERTAIN ESSENTIAL OILS are utterly essential to the workings of spells, so build up a little cache of them. Lavender is matchless in magic, exciting the passions, calming the senses, and enchanting everyone's olfactory senses. It is also useful in first aid. The best oil for getting your brain into gear is rosemary — which again has a dozen applications.

★ TRADITIONALLY, witches have used their emblematic "besom," or broom, in their magic-making. Its role is to sweep away and cleanse the environment for performing a spell, as well as to rid the house of negative thoughts. As a twenty-first-century practitioner, you might prefer to forego this picturesque status symbol in favor of the equally effective vacuum cleaner. The other quintessential witch companion, the black cat, is very much a matter of choice. I myself keep a white rabbit as a pet, and though he deports himself like a cat and naps in front of the fire, I do not think of him as my "familiar." ★ BUT THERE ARE TWO MAGICAL ITEMS WHICH YOU SHOULD HAVE. Buy a special (small) knife of good quality, tie its handle with a white or red ribbon, and hold it up to the moon the first night you bring it home, to charge it with gentle energy. Use it to cut flowers and herbs for spells, but use it only for magic (buy a second one for salads). The other vital component is a candleholder, reserved only for burning magic candles. Make it a special object and solid so it won't tip over. Glass is lovely, but metal is both representative of the elements and more durable. Silver — the precious metal of the moon — is an excellent choice. ★ A MAGIC MIRROR IS HELPFUL, but not essential. It is used to put your own "stamp" on a spell and to reflect the moon's light, thus directing her grace and blessing onto your work. A hand mirror is best, and you should charge it with the rays of the first full moon after you've bought it. Keep it in a dark-colored bag. ★ SO MUCH FOR YOUR EQUIPMENT; there are also one or two tips for good spell-making. Whenever possible, think about the phase of the moon. (There is a full list of the witch's moons in the appendix.) Try to be aware of whether the moon is waxing (growing toward full) or waning. The full moon has the height of power, but a waxing moon is desirable to work by if you want to attract something to you, whereas the waning moon is the best choice for ridding yourself of anything negative (be it a callous lover or a bad head cold). ★ FOR WORKING UP A TRULY POWERFUL SPELL, think too of the weather. If it is foggy, your spell can't travel far or fast through the ether; if it is rainy, you may feel a bit down (although water is an excellent medium for carrying magical thought); best of all is stormy weather for making magic. When all the electricity is flashing around in lightning storms and when thunder reminds us how sound carries across the earth, capitalize on the moment and get out your spell book. Borrow from the energy of the storm to charge your own battery, and you'll be amazed at the strength of your incantations.

Color breathing ★

THE USE OF COLOR IN MAGIC is just as important as the moon and the weather, and as old as the subject itself. The great Indian, Chinese, Arabic, and Western objectives of alchemy, which were originally concerned with medicine rather than the making of gold, employed the use of color tone in the hopes of altering the vibratory rates of base metals. Certainly, the effect of color on the individual psyche cannot be doubted, and we are beginning to understand the use of color in therapy for altering the mood of distressed and disturbed souls. For example, subjecting a stressed person to the color red aggravates their distress, whereas putting a hyperactive child into a pink room calms him or her down. ★ MANY MAGICAL RITUALS involve drenching the senses in color as a precursor to working magic and sending powerful thought forces. This requires a careful selection of shade to suit the job to be done: some of which is dictated, and some of which can be personal, to give the magic a sense of "signature" for the worker. For instance, if you are dealing with the area of healing, you should work in the blue/green color field, which is known to have a beneficial effect on the body's self-healing process, and then select a shade of blue or green that elicits the best response from you personally. ★ IN MATTERS OF THE HEART, there is no color quite like pink: it has an age-old association with love. The more purple there is in the pink, the more passion you are injecting. When you add in yellow, you add intellect; blue adds loyalty; and red, lust. To send greater force with your love magic, learn to breathe in the color you are working with. Light the candle(s) of your chosen color (usually, one color prescribed for the magic spell itself, and one color that is your own "signature" choice; see appendix), and inhale the feeling of the color along with any scent that might already be in the candle itself. You do this by vividly imagining the color entering your lungs, chest, head, and heart, and then gradually spreading the sense of the color down through your body, ending up right at your toes. By doing this, you are altering your own "vibratory rate" and giving yourself up to the power of the colored light. For this reason, when you want to protect yourself or anyone else, you "breathe in" pure white light, which contains all the properties of all the colors and represents the full power of the light rather than any break in the spectrum. ★ THE COLORS, OF COURSE, have a specific correspondence to numbers and strategy. This is the list you should consider when choosing an appropriate hue: Color one — initiating things — flame red. Color two — pairing off — salmon pink. Color three — groups (crowds) — amber. Color four — marriage and families — blue/ indigo. Color five — passion and action — purple/wisteria. Color six — perfect love — rose pink. Color seven — analysis — brick red. Color eight — material stability — bronze/sunshine yellow. Color nine — forgiveness — olive green. Color ten — master associations — silver. Color eleven — achieving your destiny — black and white.

Scented magic ★ I HAVE TOUCHED ON THE SUBJECT OF SCENT IN CANDLES—inhaling this

as part of the cleansing, strengthening ritual, and we have mentioned the importance of oils. The whole business of scent, furthermore, has a significant influence over our psychological awareness and the signals we emit to others; this awareness, after all, fuels a serious industry. But designer fragrances had an antecedent in floral and herbal washes (indeed, the name "lavandula," or "lavender," comes from the Latin "to wash," as no self-respecting Roman omitted this powerful ingredient from his ablutions). In days past, when streets, houses, and people existed in less sanitary conditions, anyone who understood the art of fragrancing their hair and body with the oils extracted from herbs and flowers was deemed to have magical powers over members of the opposite sex—hardly surprising, really. Thus, used with knowledge, scent is a vital component in the effects of the magic we work. ★ SOMETIMES IT IS EASIEST to choose candles for working your magic that are already imbued with fragrance: lavender to cheer the senses and excite the passions; rose to purify the environment and the psychological state of the spell; rosemary to wake up the brain and engage the mind in a high gear; melissa (lemon balm) to calm a raging anger or settle nerves; geranium to balance your mood; and so on. Often it will be worthwhile sprinkling drops of aromatic oils at the magical altars in your home, on lightbulbs, or in burners to really penetrate the physical space. Nothing is better than bathing in a cleansing bath peppered with a carefully chosen aroma to magnify the force of your magic. Even if you are sensitive to perfume, it is probable that it is the chemical used to synthesize scent that is the problem, and that subtle use of true oils—or just a gentle strewing of the herbs themselves—will be an entirely different story. In any case, consult the appendix and decide which scent matches your need, then experiment a little. ★ RELEASING POWERFUL FRAGRANCES into the air is partly what we are doing in our very first spell, which follows. It is a wonderful beginner's spell, but I do it myself to recharge my batteries every few months.

Whitest magic ★ This is a simple ritual which acts as a marvelous preparation spell

TO ALL YOUR MAGICAL WORKINGS. If you haven't got a lot of time or ingredients on hand for more complex rituals, you could do it all by itself and make any wish at all.

You will need

A compass (optional); a few drops of jasmine perfume oil (or another highly-scented white flower oil, such as gardenia or tuberose); 1 white votive or dinner candle; 1 length (12 inches [30 cm]) white ribbon

★ If you have a compass, check the direction of each cardinal point. Use your fingers to stroke some of the perfume oil gently onto the ribbon. Place your candle in a heatproof holder. Wind the ribbon around the forefinger of your dominant hand, then raise it to your temple. Bow to each of the cardinal points, beginning with north; then south; east; and west, where the sun sets. ★ Make a strong wish—to perform good, wise, powerful magic, or even just for some simple thing. Word the wish very simply, but imagine it powerfully. ★ Now light your candle, bow your head, and imagine white light spreading from you outward, coursing through your fingers, along the ribbon, to your temple, and out into the world. Think calmly; it takes only a couple of minutes. ★ Unwind the ribbon and anoint your wrists each with a drop of the perfume oil (if you are using a pure essential oil, dilute it to one-tenth of the strength in a base carrier oil first). Bow once again, quietly, to each direction, finishing with west once more. Blow out the candle and, as you do so, blow out a kiss to the world. Tie the extinguished candle at the base with the white ribbon. ★ Now you are ready for anything: for any magic making, any test of your stamina and mind, any encounter, any business. As you cross the threshold of any establishment connected with your wishes, blow a quick kiss—and be confident. ★ Remember your pledge to work only beneficent—white—magic. Everything you do will come back to you three times over. So, spread love and good humor across your patch of the globe. ★ Blessed be.

LOOKING FOR LOVE

Honoring self ★ A SPELL TO DO BEFORE ALL OTHERS. This is the best spell to begin all magic

workings and a simple one to perform. It is a good spell to use in tandem with more sophisticated rituals.

YOU WILL NEED

A photo of yourself; thin embroidery ribbons; a silver photo frame; several white votive candles

★ THE WHOLE POINT OF THIS SPELL IS THAT IT IS YOUR OWN "AUTOGRAPH," TO PRECEDE ALL OTHER SPELLS. Before you start, make yourself an altar or special place within your home which emanates radiance and love. When making your altar, choose flowers, colors, and symbols that are particularly appealing to you. ★ ON THE NIGHT OF A FULL MOON, trim your photo into a heart shape and lovingly embroider it with ribbons around the edge. Choose colors that please you and give your work a personal sense of symbolism. Chant as you work, singing a little personal song about love that you like or that you make up for yourself. ★ WHEN YOUR HANDIWORK IS COMPLETE, PLACE IT IN A FRAME AND THEN ON YOUR ALTAR. Light a candle next to the image every night until the following full moon; soon after, your luck in love will be assured.

Sowing the seed of love ★ To attract a special lover.

No one could teach the world more about love than the Italians. Following a custom my Italian grandmother taught my mother (and in the same tradition as Isabella's pot of basil in Keats's poem), this spell demonstrates how pouring your love into a little basil plant will ensure a strong love with someone.

You will need

A small pot; some earth; some basil seeds

★ On a waxing moon in late spring or summer, take a few basil seeds and sow them carefully in one or two small pots or containers. As you sow them, sing a sweet song or think loving thoughts, and feel love entering your life. Water the seeds lovingly each day until they germinate, saying as you do: *"Sono innamorata. Grazie."* When the seedlings appear, take great care of them, especially if the weather is cold (in which case you will need a very sunny draft-free window). You mustn't let them die, and never use these special plants for cooking, for they are sacred to love. ★ You will meet a special love within a few months — perhaps the love of your life.

My good friend and former neighbor Zoe did this spell to excellent effect many years ago, just before she met her present husband. She chose a Greek yogurt pot for the container; rather amazingly, when she met him, she discovered he had lived for many years in Greece. We did our magic together, and she nursed the seedlings on her sunny windowsill. The power must have been strong, for I, too, met my future husband a few months later.

A seashore spell ★

To ATTRACT A FOREIGN LOVER. There has always been something glamorous and superior about a love affair with a foreigner. If you have drunk from the cup of holiday romance before, but prefer that this time he should come to you, plan a trip to the seashore and see what you can do to influence the fates.

YOU WILL NEED

A seashell; a lock of your hair; a small silver charm; a sprig of rosemary; a small piece of paper; a red ribbon or cord;
sealing wax; a flask of wine; your magic mirror

★ WHEN THE MOON IS NEWEST AND THE EVENING LONG, JOURNEY TO A QUIET SEASHORE. In a pouch carry the above, tokens of your love, and at day's end sit by the water's edge facing the rising moon. Breathe in the salty fragrance and imagine your life filled with love, with the partner you hope might be your companion. Hold the talismans in your outstretched hands: the shell, symbol of the traveler; the lock of your own hair to represent your thoughts and your true self; a silver charm for luck (silver is sacred to the moon; formerly, in Britain, a sixpence would have been used); and the sprig of rosemary, token of love and sacred in sea spells.

★ ASK THE MOON TO SEEK FOR YOU THE ONE BEST QUALIFIED TO APPRECIATE YOUR WISE MIND AND LOVING HEART AND, WHEN SHE HAS FOUND HIM, TO SEND HIM ON HIS JOURNEY TO FIND YOU. Now write your name on paper and wrap it into a scroll with the red cord, then seal it with the wax and show it to the moon and the sea. Sip wine from the flask and toast the moon, mistress of the sea and our emotional tides, and the nighttime companion of us all. Take the air, sea, and sky into your mind, try to become one with them, and watch the tide lapping onto the shore, seeing it bringing your beloved right to your feet.

★ NOW WHISPER NINE TIMES: *"Shine your light across the ocean, / Guide to me my love's devotion, / He who's known another life, / May now make of me his wife."* While you are chanting, cast the scroll into the water. Before you lose sight of it, hold your mirror up to the moon to catch her light and then to the ocean so that it glimpses your scroll in its glass. Take the shell, rosemary, and lock of your hair in one hand, and in the other hand offer the silver token up to the moon, inviting her blessing. Make a small hole in the sand or pebbles beside the water with your hand and place herb, hair, and shell in it. Splash a drop of wine into the hole, cover it again, and lay your head on top of the mound for just a moment. Now you have asked the earth, too, to help. ★ YOUR MAGIC AT THE SEASHORE IS COMPLETE. When you return home, hold the silver charm up to the moon again to bring your magic into your dwelling place, and stand a broom in any corner of your home. For a month, show the silver to the moon each night and sleep with it under your pillow. ★ WITHIN ONE TO THREE MONTHS, YOUR FOREIGNER SHOULD HAVE APPEARED.

The band of violets ★ MOST BEAUTIFUL OF THE MANY LEGENDS OF THE VIOLET IS

THAT OF CUPID, WHO LOOSES HIS BOW IN LOVE UPON A STARRY MAIDEN; his arrow, missing its mark, falls instead upon a patch of milk-white violets, turning them gradually, in rings from the center outward, from white to the more familiar passionate purple we know today. This features in Shakespeare's *A Midsummer Night's Dream,* when Oberon instructs Puck to collect the juice of the flower and sprinkle it on Titania's eyelids so that she will fall in love with the first person she sees on waking. To loose your fiery arrow into the darkness and find a lover, follow the adaptation below of his spell: *"Yet marked I where the bolt of Cupid fell. It fell upon a little western flower — Before, milk-white; now, purple with love's wound."*

YOU WILL NEED

⅓ cup violet flowers (dried or fresh); 2 fluid ounces goat's milk; a small candle, either violet colored or violet scented; a posy of fresh violets for working into a band for the hair or a necklace

★ ON THE VERY FIRST NIGHT OF A NEW MOON, steep the violet flowers in the milk for an hour. While they are steeping, make a circle of the fresh violets with the candle in the center and light it, saying: *"Cupid loose your fiery brand, / May this flower be Love's command!"* Now, in front of the glowing candle, bathe your face with the violet-scented milk (don't be alarmed; it makes an excellent skin tonic). Picture yourself seated in the midst of a ring of white flowers gradually turning purple with the onset of love; imagine love coloring your own life in this way. Complete the spell by weaving the violets into a daisy-chain-like band, big enough for a necklace or a chaplet for your hair. ★ ON THE DAY FOLLOWING YOUR MAGIC-WORKING, WEAR THE FLOWERS ALL DAY, repeating the words above softly from time to time. By the time of the full moon you should be fending off interested parties, and within the month, you will have met someone very special indeed.

If violets are truly scarce, you could use just one flower, placed in front of the candle, and put it into a locket which you would then wear in place of the garland of flowers. This has the added advantage of becoming a long-term love token.

23

Pensées de moi ★ FOR THOSE WHO HAVE BEEN DISAPPOINTED IN LOVE. If yours is a story

of always attracting the wrong person, and your heart has been broken once too often, this spell is for you. It will heal the wounds of past mistakes and lay the groundwork for a new beginning in your love life.

YOU WILL NEED

Pansy seeds; a small terra cotta pot or window box; earth and a small trowel; paper with your name written on it; some of your nail filings

★ THE PANSY (OR HEARTSEASE) HAS LONG BEEN THE FAVORITE OF THOSE WHOSE HEARTS NEED HEALING. Grow yours to put sorrow behind you and prepare for a happier future. ★ THIS SPELL IS BEST PERFORMED ON VALENTINE'S DAY (FEBRUARY 14), BELTANE (MAY 1), MIDSUMMER DAY (JUNE 21), OR LAMMAS (AUGUST 1). Plant your seeds lovingly on one of the days mentioned, first putting the piece of paper with your name on it into the earth. Water in the seeds and scatter your nail filings on top. Tend your plant with care, and when the first flower blooms, pick it on a waning moon and press it in a favorite book of love poetry. Keep it with you always to attract love. ★ CHOOSE A MAINLY YELLOW FLOWER IF YOU WANT AN INTELLECTUAL MATCH, RICH PURPLE IF YOU SEEK PASSION, OR SOFT BLUE IF YOU LONG FOR A LOVE THAT IS SIMPLE YET TRUE.

Nos amoureux, assis par terre,
Commencèrent à deviser,
Entre le rire et le baiser,
D'un bon dîner qu'ils y ...
En ce lieu même, à le ... loisir,
La place leur devenait chère,
Il leur fallait y revenir.
Tout ... sous la verdure,
... aventure,
... buisson.
... garçon
... ore;
... langer,
...

Et le voir s'en all...
Sans adieu, plain...
Tremblante elle ...
Croyant qu'il s'é...
Dans quelque ...
Et le serra tout...
Non plus en a...
Qu'eût-elle fa...
Habitués à la...
Gardent jusc...
Leur unique...
Mais la mo...
Déjà le sp...

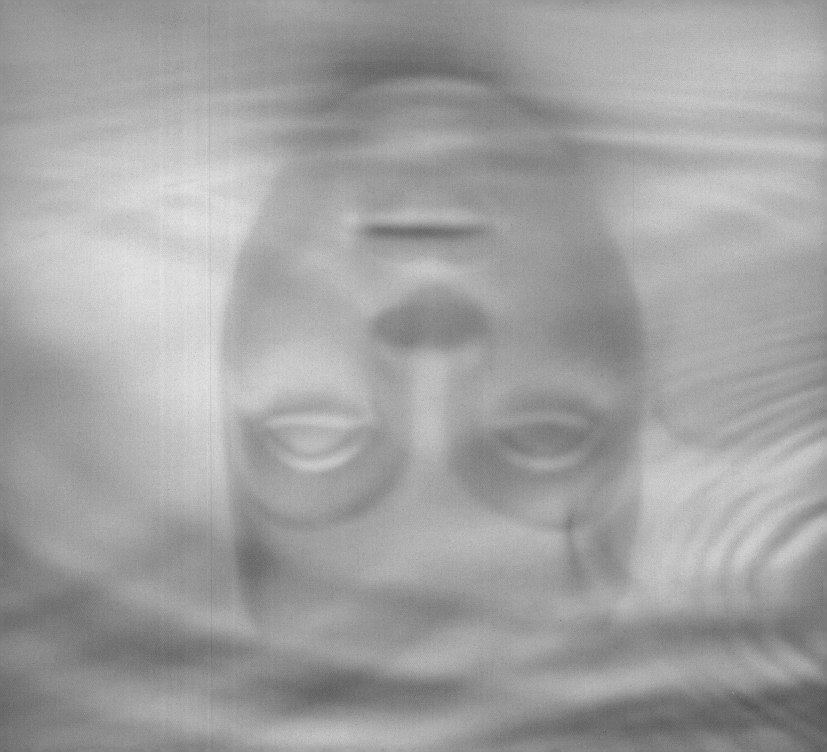

Divine intervention ★ By reading the signs of the fates, you may discover

YOUR LIFE PARTNER. ★ AT FIRST LIGHT ON EASTER SUNDAY, VISIT THE WELL AT CERNE ABBAS, IN DORSET, ENGLAND OR ANOTHER ANCIENT SPRING TO CATCH A GLIMPSE OF YOUR FUTURE WIFE OR HUSBAND REFLECTED IN THE WATER. ★ BRUSH YOUR HAIR IN FRONT OF A MIRROR ON ST. AGNES'S EVE (JANUARY 19), VALENTINE'S DAY (FEBRUARY 14), OR HALLOWEEN (OCTOBER 31), and you will see the face of your future partner mysteriously reflected in the glass. ★ PLACE A HAZELNUT OR APPLE SEED IN THE EMBERS OF THE FIRE ON HALLOWEEN OR AT YULE (DECEMBER 21/22), AND SAY THESE WORDS: *"If you love me pop and fly; if not, lie still and die."* If the lover that you have in mind as you say this is the one for you, the nut will pop in the fire; if not, it will stay mute. ★ PLACE ALL THE LETTERS OF THE ALPHABET ON INDIVIDUAL PIECES OF PAPER FACE DOWNWARD IN A BASIN OF WATER BEFORE YOU GO TO BED ON MIDSUMMER EVE (JUNE 20). The letter that turns over during the night will be the initial of your true love/wife/husband. ★ IF YOU HAVE SOMEONE IN YOUR HEART, CARVE THEIR INITIALS INTO A LEAF AND PLACE IT IN YOUR SHOE OVERNIGHT. In the morning, if the initials are clearer they'll marry you; if not, they won't. ★ PEEL AN APPLE IN ONE UNBROKEN PIECE AND THROW THE PEEL OVER YOUR SHOULDER; it will fall in the shape of the first letter of your intended's name. ★ IF THREE UNMARRIED PEOPLE WITH THE SAME NAME SIT AT A TABLE AND ALL SAY *"White Horses,"* one of them will be married within the year. ★ SEW A PIECE OF YARROW INTO A FLANNEL POUCH AND PLACE IT UNDER YOUR PILLOW. Say these words: *"Thou pretty herb of Venus's tree, / Thy certain name is yarrow; / Now who my lifelong partner be, / Pray tell thou me tomorrow."* Your dream will reveal your true love. ★ IF YOU WISH FOR A LOVE WITH A NUTMEG IN YOUR PALM OR POCKET, he or she will be older than you. ★ THE FIRST NEW MOON OF THE NEW YEAR, VIEWED THROUGH A HANDKERCHIEF, WILL REVEAL THE NUMBER OF YEARS YOU will have to wait before marriage. ★ STIR A FIRE WITH A POKER; if it burns bright on repetition of your lover's name, the love affair will grow. ★ BEFORE BED, ASK: *"New moon, new moon, hail to thee; this night may I my true love see."* Walk backward to bed, watching the moon all the while, and the name or a picture of your future love will appear in your dreams. ★ SCATTER FLOUR OR TALC UNDER A ROSEMARY BUSH ON BELTANE (MAY 1) OR HALLOWEEN, AND LOOK FOR THE INITIALS OF YOUR FUTURE LOVE TRACED IN IT.

TWO'S COMPANY

The ribbon of love 1 ★ To bewitch him with thoughts of only you.

You have become practiced now in the force of thought required to work your magic, so you should be quite adept enough to try this excellent little spell.

You will need

1 yard of red ribbon

★ During the day, as many times as you can find a spare five or ten minutes, go to a quiet spot and wrap the length of ribbon around your right index finger. Put it to your "third eye" (between your eyebrows) and concentrate on your love with all your might: vividly imagine the smell, touch, and feel of every part of his body, from the tip of his toe to the top of his head (lingering on his lips as you go). Mischievously ask him to think of you, and try to hold the image and thought for five minutes — harder than you think. Repeat several times during the day, and over the course of at least a week. *Whenever possible, sleep with the red ribbon under your shared pillow.*

Three woven ribbons to strengthen the bond

★ This spell is best performed on St. Agnes's Eve (January 19) or Valentine's Eve (February 13).

You will need

3 ribbons, each 15 inches long: 1 pink, 1 lavender, and 1 white; a vanilla pod

★ Tie the three ribbons together by a knot in the top, saying your partner's name and your name and asking the help of Venus or Isis. Speaking the three names as you go, make the ribbons into a beautiful braid, and secure the end with another knot. Place the ribbons to your heart and wish your loved one "only good." Now wind the braid gently but firmly around the vanilla pod. ★ This love charm is special for you and your partner; you should keep it with you, especially when you meet each other, and sleep on it at night. If you are right for each other, he will soon declare himself.

Golden slumbers ★ THIS SPELL HAS A LONG HISTORY IN THE HARDIE FAMILY and is held

in much affection by its younger branch. Like "Bound together" on page 38, it employs an element of subterfuge, but it is fail-safe in eliciting declarations of love and often some little luck with money as well.

YOU WILL NEED

A golden coin in current circulation; blue flowers, such as daisies, hyacinths, or bluebells

★ PLACE THE GOLDEN COIN BETWEEN YOUR PALMS AND MAKE A PRAYER (ADDRESS WHOMEVER YOU FEEL COMFORTABLE WITH) FOR LOVE TO RISE IN A GREAT WAVE AND FLOOD YOUR LIFE and that of the person you love with great happiness. Now take the coin and imagine your loved one's face thereon. Carry it to a circle that you have made up from the blue flowers, and place it in the center of the ring. Leave it there on the night of the full moon, and in the morning take it to your love. You must contrive that he or she shall have it, perhaps to buy something on an errand for you. Once the coin (and it must be this very coin) has left your beloved's hands in a gesture of unselfishness, a display of deep affection will be forthcoming. In my experience this has always come before the next full moon. **Philip gave his coin to the lovely Lauren during the early days of their attraction; she, in turn, bought a scratcher in a small lottery with it. Enough money was gained to buy them both a wonderful dinner, and at this dinner their love affair moved onto an altogether higher plateau.**

33

The manicure ★ A LITTLE ADDITIVE TO HIS OR HER COFFEE BREAK.

You will need

Some nail filings from your recipient (as opposed to dominant) hand; a cup of freshly made tea or coffee

★ WASH YOUR HANDS THOROUGHLY BEFORE YOU BEGIN. Chanting as you work, file your nails into his or her cup, saying these words: *"Let me nail your true intent, / Show me if your heart is sent, / Straight to me without lament."* Add those little calorie-free filings without malice and without trying to bind your love to you. The sipper will soon come forward if he or she is truly interested.

"Six flowers, six charms, six scented balms"

★ UTILIZING THE NUMBER SIX (THE NUMBER OF LOVE), the following spell employs lucky charms, flowers, and scents to map out the initials of the one you desire. This is prepared at an altar of love, to nudge flirtatious affairs toward consummation.

You will need

Some pink velvet or silk; a pink candle; 6 flowers of any type, but pink in color; 6 small flower vases; 6 charms taken from the list on pages 154–157; 6 drops of different aromatic oils of your choice, to anoint the objects

★ PREPARE YOUR ALTAR BY DRAPING THE FABRIC ACROSS IT, then burn a pink candle and address the goddess, asking for her help. Do this for several days before performing the spell itself. ★ PLACE THE FLOWERS IN THE VASES AND ANOINT THE CHARMS, then make the shape of your lover's initials by alternating vases and charms. Place the index finger of your dominant hand to your brow (beribboned in red or royal blue, if you like), and concentrate on your question of fidelity or sincerity to your initialed love. Inhale the scents and dab a little on yourself the next six times you see your love. On the seventh occasion, passion will burst forth, or, if the designated love is a callous playboy/girl, the love affair will wither away.

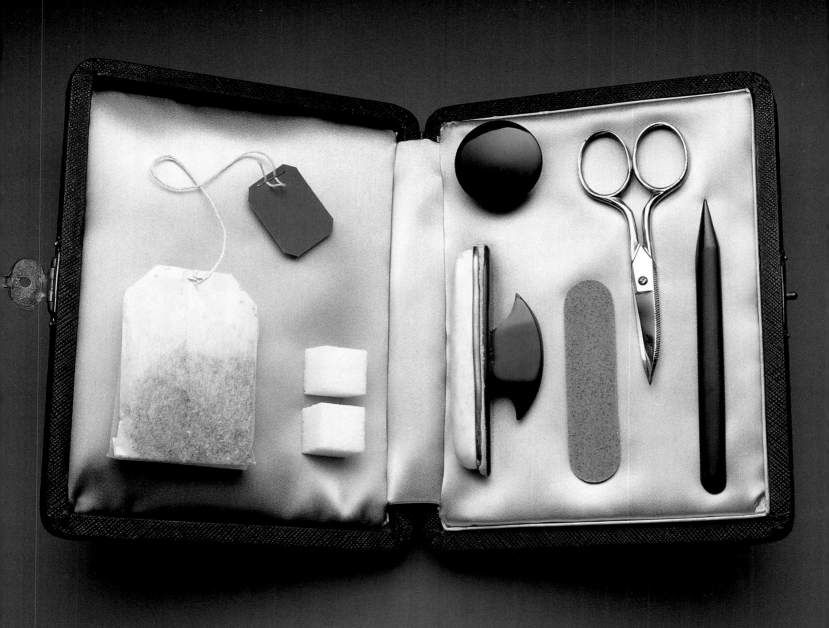

The pansy offering ★ IF SOMEONE YOU ARE STRONGLY ATTRACTED TO HAS BEEN

BUZZING AROUND YOU LIKE A BEE, going out with you on an irregular basis, or simply confusing you with signals of deep passion followed by indifference, this is the spell for you.

YOU WILL NEED

White or pink votive candles; 1 yard of purple ribbon and 1 yard of yellow ribbon; a photograph each of you and the person you love, approximately passport sized, and with a clear likeness of the face; a yellow and purple pansy of the "face" variety (unlike the solid-colored, these usually have a tri-colored effect and look like a little clownish face); a wooden bowl of water, scented with a few drops of either bergamot or clary sage oil

★ BEFORE YOU BEGIN THIS SPELL, TAKE THE TROUBLE TO DO A "CLEANSING REGIME" IN YOUR HOME. Using a broom or a vacuum cleaner, physically sweep through the house, starting from the center and working toward the front door. Work up as much physical energy as possible. Now light the votive candles at strategic places in your home, saying, *"Blessings be to this place"* as you light each one. This should help to alter your outlook so that you become calm and serene. Wind the two ribbons around the index finger of your right hand, hold it to your forehead, and concentrate on the image of your love. ★ NOW BREATHE THE COLORS OF THE PANSY, JUST AS YOU WOULD A CANDLE, AND PLACE IT BETWEEN PHOTOS OF YOU AND YOUR LOVER, with the photos facing in toward the flower. Hold the photos and pansy between your two hands for a moment, as in prayer, and ask that honesty and fidelity visit your union. Talk to your love as though he or she were there. Say what you would wish to say about not trampling your heart with indiscretions to others if his or her love for you is serious. Ask that if there is any possibility of a deep and lasting affection between you, he or she should by all means be playful, but stop playing games with your heart.

★ NOW TAKE THE RIBBONS FROM YOUR FINGER AND WIND THEM TOGETHER AROUND THE PHOTOS AND PANSY, SANDWICHED TOGETHER. As you wind, say: *"If your love be true and dear, / Make you your intentions clear."* Finish the sandwich with a tiny bow of both colors. Place the package beside or in front of the wooden dish filled with water. Put all the objects near an open window, somewhere they may remain undisturbed for seven days. Each time you pass the bowl, repeat the words of the spell. The following week the relationship will show its true direction.

Bound together ★ RIBBONS AND CORDS HAVE POWERFUL MAGIC WORK TO DO IN REVEALING

AND HOLDING IN PLACE FRAGILE GROWING FEELINGS BETWEEN NEW COURTING COUPLES. I love this ribbon spell for its sheer playfulness and its "espionage" elements. It is, however, loving and harmless and draws on nothing sinister or worrisome for your loved one. Perform it with humor, but in safety.

YOU WILL NEED

The longest salmon pink candle you can find; 1 yard of white or blue ribbon, ¼ inch in width

★ TAKE YOUR CANDLE AND TIE IT WITH THE RIBBON, all the way from top to bottom, tying it into a pretty bow at the base end. As you bind, say your loved one's name over and over, and ask your wish of Venus with the following words: *"I mean him (her) no harm, / Bid him (her) take no alarm, / May our love be a balm, / To heal and to calm."* Light the candle for a few minutes, being careful not to let the ribbon catch fire, and repeat your prayer to Venus several times. Now extinguish the candle with laughter and warmth, unbind the ribbon, hold it across your open palms, and send a beam of love and cheerfulness to your beloved. ★ THE NEXT PIECE OF THE SPELL REQUIRES A LITTLE INVENTIVENESS. You must take the ribbon to the one you like so much and carefully slip it into his or her pocket, or briefcase, or car. If you are discovered later, you can say it is a ribbon of protection, but try to get it there undetected. Almost miraculously, the relationship can move on to its next phase.

THREE'S A CROWD

★ Before performing any of the following spells, it is very important to examine your motives and make certain that you are not trying to cause havoc in a current and working relationship. If you do not honor this code, the results will eventually be to your detriment. Remember, magic and the Wiccan path urge us to use the life force to attract and generate our own happiness, not someone else's sadness! ★ Preface each spell with a candle-burning ceremony, cleansing the room and your thoughts of anything negative or sad. For this, breathe in the color pink of the love candle and add amber, preferably by utilizing a piece of amber, to dispel the effects of the "crowding" of your relationship.

Bite the dust ★ Or actually, sand! If your loved one shows every sign of being happy with you but cannot quite let go of a past relationship, try this seaside ritual.

You will need

2 small pieces of high-quality flexible paper, such as rice paper or parchment; a pair of nail clippers

★ You must perform this spell at sundown on a beach, even if this means waiting until your vacation. On one piece of paper write the name of the one you love; on the other, the name of his or her love from the past. Make a little knot of the names, tying them together. Look at them in the palm of your hand, and say: *"I respect and understand that you have been that with each other which was tender and close; / But if your love be truly over, consign it to the past and move on."* Now bury the pieces of paper in the sand with the nail clippers, and ask that affairs be manicured, trimmed, and tidied up. ★ Stand now, bow to the setting sun, and ask blessings of Venus, whose star will shortly rise. Ask that she may bestow on the other party a happy and a worthwhile love — in short, that he or she may find happiness elsewhere. Ask, too, that the past be now the past, and that the future belong to you. Kneel again on the sand and say: *"So mote it be."* ★ You must now release your own doubts about the past relationship. Regard the magic as already effective, and let no doubts haunt you from here on.

Letting go ★ The pansy, or heartsease, rules again in this next spell, this time creating

A RING OF PROTECTION AND POWER TO DRIVE OFF UNLUCKY OR UNHEALTHY LOVE. You could use violets instead, for these have many properties in common with the pansy.

You will need

Some hard apple cider (buy a commercial cider if you wish, but infuse it with extra power by adding fresh apple rings); an oak cleansing bath (see page 138); a ring, about 1 yard in circumference, of pansies or violets

★ Drink your cider in the cleansing bath, imagining all cares washing from your body. Feel the warmth of the bath penetrating your very essence, and think of this as an omen of new warmth in a future life. Toast the moon and the goddess with your cider, and when you have finished your bath, tip a little cider into the roots of an oak or other tree near your house, offering a libation to the wood spirits who may cleanse your world. Finally, sit in the midst of the fairy flower ring and pray for new growth in the one special relationship you wish to move forward. Sit long enough to be circumspect about past errors, and be clear about your intentions for future happiness. Pledge also to spread this new-found happiness among your friends. ★ This spell works wonders if you cannot let go of a past love affair by yourself.

The healed heart ★ When your partner has been hurt in love more times than you can count and has lost all heart for a secure future, employ "heartsease" to turn the tide of his or her luck.

You will need

A plain blue or creamy-white pansy (one color only, save for the "eye"); some beautiful (perhaps handmade) paper, pink, oat, or white in color; some calligraphy pens; a picture of the loved one or a lock of his or her hair; a pinch of ground orrisroot; a white or blue candle to match the flower

★ You must begin this spell by pressing the pansy (heartsease) to your bosom. Imagine it quickly cleansing away the pain, then infusing color and hope into your beloved's heart. Keep the pansy, and before the next full moon make a pansy mandala. Draw a wheel on your paper, placing the pansy and the picture of your lover or lock of his or her hair right in the center. Secure it with a little glue, and sprinkle orrisroot over it. Now, around the flowery center, carefully write a prayer to release your loved one from past pains. Use your own words, but make sure they are a sincere and unselfish reflection of your wish to see the person happier — hopefully, with you. Include the full name and birthdate of your loved one, and the words *"Amor vincit omnia"* ("Love conquers all"). Finally, cover your mandala with some tissue paper and place it for safekeeping in an envelope or plastic folder. ★ On the night of the next full moon, take the precious mandala to a candle, which you light with these same words: *"Amor vincit omnia"*; then, pass the mandala through the candlelight. Imagine your love free from darkness and loneliness, shedding the confusion and sadness of times past. Finally, place the mandala in a safe place, such as a photo album, with a picture of your love or with a letter or card received from him or her. Keep it always.

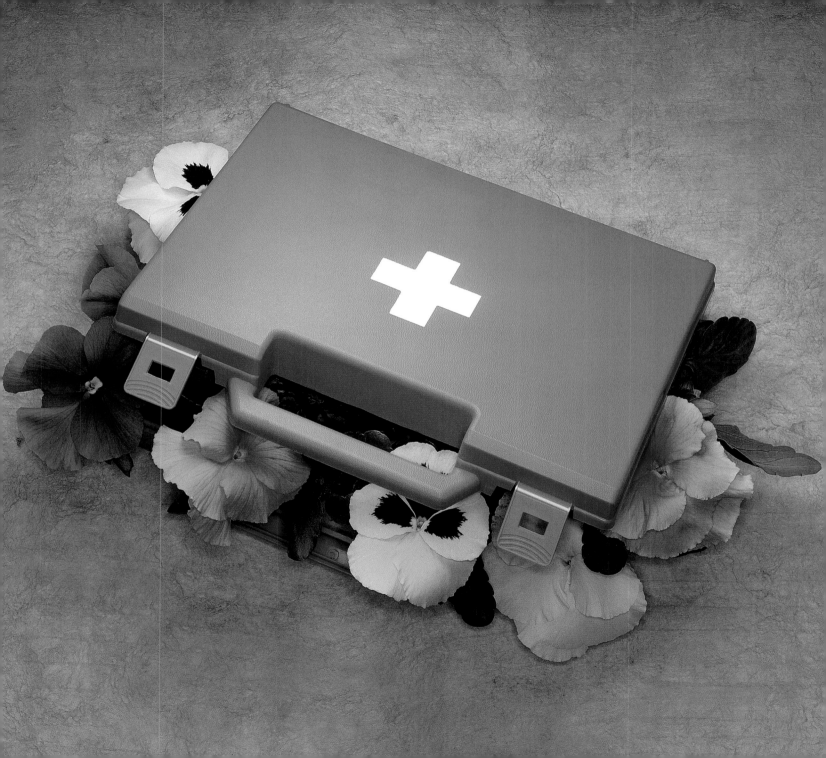

Cast adrift ★ PERHAPS THE LOVE AFFAIR YOU HAVE WITH YOUR OTHERWISE PERFECT MATE IS BEING

HINDERED BY THE "PRESENCE" OF A PAST LOVE WHO IS MORE APPEALING THROUGH ABSENCE. If the specter of a previous lover haunts your happiness, here's how to turn the tide.

YOU WILL NEED

2 little handmade boats, such as a child would make from paper or card stock, but strong enough to be, if not seaworthy, then at least riverworthy; paints and markers to decorate the boats; a photo or drawing of your partner with his or her previous love

★ THE MORE CARE YOU PUT INTO THE DESIGN AND EXECUTION OF THESE BOATS, THE MORE POWERFUL WILL BE YOUR MAGIC-WORKING. One boat should be named after your love and the other after his or her past lover, the names painted or carefully marked so as to be reasonably waterproof. Place an object belonging to your loved one in his or her boat, and something belonging to your rival (if available) in his or hers. Using a picture of the erstwhile couple, make a little flag, cut it in half, and glue one half to each boat. Lastly, to the boat named for your love, add your name in the form of another flag. ★ ON THE FULL MOON, TAKE YOUR BOATS TO THE WATER'S EDGE AND KNEEL. Praying for happiness for all the parties named, ask that the past love release your love and allow everyone to move on with their lives. Make sure to wish your rival happiness in a new life. Now launch the boats, facing them away from one another. Watch for a while to see if they set sail in opposite directions. Urge the elements to separate them if this is just. After a short space you will know if you have any hope of seeing them go their different ways. If your boat sails well, your hopes should soon be riding the crest of a new wave.

Shirley has performed this spell on many occasions for her man, for his past memories and pain are deep. However, she is tremendously kind, patient, and persistent, and has secured more happiness with him than did any of her previous rivals. They battle along on the high seas, and no one deserves greater happiness—which will yet come in full measure.

★ THERE ARE TWO POWERFUL SPELLS YOU MIGHT CONSIDER IF THE PROBLEMS YOU FACE ARE BECAUSE OF A THIRD PARTY. In a bona fide situation where your partner is being wooed away by the "unscrupulous mistress/lover" figure, I think it is perfectly correct to put your own fighting energies out into the cosmos and ask the gods to favor you with victory. However, be warned: You may be able to fool yourself about your motives, but if you are trying to bind a person to you against their will and putting a negative vibration onto someone else in the process, you will get this back in threefold measure. It is not worth the consequences. So, unless your heart and motives are completely fair, leave these spells alone.

The mad tea party ★ A SPELL TO TEST THE STRENGTH OF HIS OR HER AFFECTION.

YOU WILL NEED

A cup of tea or coffee; your nail filings

★ MAKE HIM A CUP OF COFFEE OR TEA, AND PUT SOME OF YOUR NAIL FILINGS INTO HIS CUP TO REMIND HIM OF THE ESSENCE OF YOU. My mother swore by this spell for protecting her relationship.

Freezing off a rival ★ A SPELL TO DETER A THIRD PARTY.

YOU WILL NEED

A small piece of paper with the name of your rival written on it; a tiny envelope; sealing wax;
a small plastic container; spring water

★ PERFORM THIS SPELL ON A WANING MOON, NOT FAR PAST FULL. Pop the piece of paper into a tiny envelope (gift card size), then seal it with sealing wax. As you do this, say over and over that you mean the person (address them by name) no harm and wish them absolute luck in love with someone else, but not with your partner. Send them warm feelings, and ask that they retreat from their pursuit of your beloved. Now place the envelope into the container and top with spring water, saying again, *"I mean you no harm, but spare my love your charm."* Place the container in the freezer, and ask a blessing on your magic. If this is merely an interloper, and not in fact your lover's real soulmate in your stead, the powers of her attraction will steadily wane.

★ BE CONFIDENT, AND DO NOT RESORT TO SNIDE REMARKS IN THE MEANTIME.

TYING THE KNOT

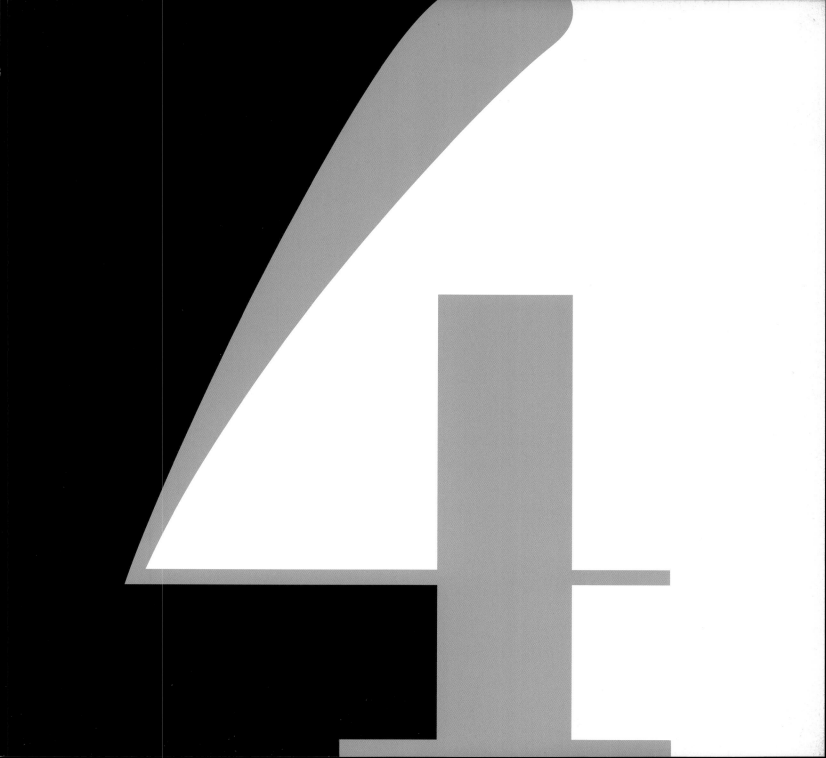

Bright white light ★ Preparation for marital magic is a serious business.

It is recommended that you perform this spell as a prelude to each other spell from this chapter. It is like making proper homemade pastry to go on a magnificent pie—so please don't omit this.

You will need

A photo of you and your lover together; 4 blue/indigo and 4 white votive candles

★ Start by concentrating your thought forces on the photo. Generate energy from your fingertips and toes and imagine a great white light starting from you and filling the room, encircling the photograph as it gains power. Through the white light, tell your loved one what a formidable couple you are, and how much stronger you would be together in the world if united. Send the idea of your union lots of love: surround the "couple" with light and power. Now place the photo in the midst of the candles, which should form a ring, alternating indigo and white. Light them clockwise, and swirl your love around your partner.

Love adorned

You will need

A tarot card representing Arcanum VI, "The Lovers"; 2 different-colored ribbons, each 1 yard long; a needle with a large eye; a beautiful box padded with feathers (like a nesting box)

★ Choose the colors of the ribbons to represent you and your love (choose your favorite colors, if you like). Lovingly embroider the tarot card however you wish with the ribbons. As you work, imagine embroidering your relationship with sunshine, light, color, and love. Make sure that the colors interweave, and tie off the ends securely in a small knot. Now write your names, preferably in calligraphy (intricately interwoven, if you like) around the card. Place the tarot card in a box softened with feathers and send it a final blast of vibrant light before "putting it to bed." Cherish it. Proposals will follow.

The walnut shell ★ Since Roman times, walnuts have been symbols of nuptial

BLISS. This is largely because within the shell the nut divides perfectly into two entities. Nuts are also symbols of fertility and a high-protein food. The lovely spell that follows is possibly an adaptation from Roman times, and anticipates the walnuts' being used to make the "marriage bread" (wedding cake).

YOU WILL NEED

About 12 walnuts, whole in their shells; a pouch made of 4 colors of velvet—to your own design if possible; a drawing or photograph of you together as a couple; a blossomed bower, traditionally strewn with petals of orange blossom, but rose or fruit blossom petals are also suitable

★ USING THE WALNUTS, TRACE THE INITIALS OF YOUR BELOVED'S NAME UNDER A TREE OR IN A QUIET CORNER OF THE PLACE WHERE YOU LIVE. Lay your hands over the letters/walnuts and infuse as much love and strength as you can into them. Imagine scenes of children dancing, a May dance, you and others bedecked with flowers and ribbons—in short, a marriage ceremony. Let the initials stand while you sew up your velvet pouch, which must be big enough to contain all the nuts. When you have finished, put the photo of both of you into the pouch, then put the walnuts on top. Close the bag with a ribbon or drawstring and walk it in procession to your "bower." (If you live in the city, make up your bower in a corner of your apartment by creating a leafy haven and strewing the area with your chosen petals. Do not disturb it once you have created it.) ★ THE POUCH MUST NOW PASS 30 DAYS IN THE BOWER. Each day around 11:00 A.M. and 3:00 P.M., hold your palms toward it and close your eyes for a moment. The spell is "closed" by placing the pouch in a coat, a bag, or a treasure box, and sweeping (not vacuuming, please) the petals out of the house or bower. They must be returned to earth, so toss them on the ground. ★ WITHIN 30 DAYS TO 30 WEEKS (CERTAINLY WITHIN THE YEAR), THE BUSINESS OF YOUR MARRIAGE WILL BE DISCUSSED.   **Gabriele and Deborah have a garden full of blossoming trees, and a beechwood bowl of walnuts forever in their house, in deference to this spell.**

57

Pressing your suit ★ A tasty trick to win over your lover. Ginger is a spice whose

properties have long been prized. In medieval times, there was a tradition of making ginger cakes and cookies, often in the shape of a playing card, and decorating them with gold leaf for feasts and fairs on holy days. The hearts suit was the popular choice, its ace being an invitation to love. The deuce might indicate a marriage proposal. The other cards in the suit were sometimes picked by young girls "blind" as a kind of divination—getting the king or the knave meant that you would meet someone special at the fair itself. If you want to make one of these beautiful treats and keep it for yourself for luck in love, choose the nine; but, if you want to give one to your love to excite his or her senses or to progress the love affair, the ace must be your choice.

You will need

Your favorite recipe for ginger cookies, to which you should add 1 or 2 drops cassia food oil; 1 sheet of edible gold leaf for decorating

★ Make your recipe with the cassia added. While the cookies are still warm, add the gold leaf in the decorative pattern of your choice, following the manufacturer's instructions.

The red candle ★

To be performed on a Friday, this spell uses red, the color of action, to get an inert romance moving toward the altar.

You will need

A lock of your lover's hair; a bowl of the herb yarrow; a red votive candle; any piece of jewelery given to you by your loved one

★ On the chosen Friday of a new moon, place a lock of your love's hair into a bowl of yarrow, which is an extremely potent magical herb with a very soothing fragrance. Bow your head and ask for earnest love; ask that if this relationship be not destined for growth and future happiness, that it reveal itself thus, allowing you to find a suitable partner with whom to settle.

★ Now light the votive candle and pass the jewel through the space above the flame. Repeat: *"Amor gignit amorem."* Let the candle burn down, repeating these words often, and keep candle, bowl, jewel, hair, and yarrow in proximity to each other for a month. Thereafter things will improve one way or another.

The brooch ★

A brooch set with the loved one's hair was a trusted amulet and keepsake in Victorian times. If you can find a jeweler to work with you on this, it makes powerful magic.

You will need

A lock of your lover's hair; a lock of your own hair; a specially made locket or brooch

★ Weave the strands of hair into a beautiful love knot. Sometimes they look attractive made into an intertwined pair of initials. Take your prize to a jeweler, who should set them into a specially made locket or brooch, usually covered with glass. When you receive the brooch back, take it to the moon of the first night and the sun of the following day, and ask: *"Enlighten our lives; / May our nights share ever after the hours of the moon, and our days the hours of the sun; / May our two lives, and our two souls, now be as one."* Within three months, you should be setting a date.

The myrtle mantle ★ Myrtle was a favorite of the Victorians and was used

IN THE QUEEN'S WEDDING BOUQUET but its pedigree as a love talisman is older, for the Greeks and Romans thought it the property of Aphrodite (Venus). Winners at Olympic games wore it and so should you, if you would gain your prize.

You will need

Some myrtle flowers and leaves; a coat worn by your love and one of your own; some boughs of myrtle for an altar; 7 small lavender-scented candles (one for each day of the week)

★ SEW SOME LEAVES AND FLOWERS INTO THE POCKETS OF YOUR FAVORITE COAT AND, WHILE FEIGNING SOME REPAIRS, SEW SOME INTO THE POCKET OF YOUR PARTNER'S. It can be a well-loved jacket or an overcoat, and the addition need not be very bulky. Now prepare an altar of myrtle, laying a fresh cloth and placing boughs of the plant across it. Amid the greenery place a candle, lavender scented or anointed with lavender oil. Light the candle at moonrise, saying: *"Better we wed over the myrtle than over the moor."* (Better to marry the one you know than a stranger!) Wish for married peace and harmony. Let the candle burn awhile. ★ EVERY NIGHT OF THE WEEK, REPLACE THE CANDLE WITH A FRESH ONE, repeat the words, and stroke the leaves of the plant to release its fragrance. A proposal must surely follow.

AND BABY MAKES
THREE

The parsley diet ★ To aid conception. The ingredients in this spell have a long tradition

of use in aiding fertility and are excellent for female hormones.

You will need

Fresh flat-leaf parsley; cucumbers; lettuce; fennel bulb; sunflower seeds; pine nuts, hazelnuts and walnuts; fresh basil leaves

★ FROM THE MOMENT YOU DECIDE YOU WISH TO BECOME PREGNANT, INCLUDE THESE INGREDIENTS IN A DAILY SALAD, TOGETHER WITH WHATEVER OTHER INGREDIENTS YOU LIKE. At the same time, start growing some parsley in your garden or on your windowsill, and pat the earth around it each day, asking for the blessing of Mother Earth. This can be a very effective ritual for some.

Oak and mistletoe: the royal marriage ★ You may

WISH TO PERFORM ONE OF THESE RATHER MORE SYMBOLIC RITUALS AT THE SAME TIME AS YOUR PARSLEY DIET. Oak, and the mistletoe that grew in its branches, were sacred above all else to the Druids, who knew their powers. The acorn is a strong talisman of fertility and increased sexual powers; some say it can even cure impotence. ★ FIND TWO ACORNS AND POUR A FEW DROPS OF ALE OR WINE OVER THE ROOTS OF THE OAK TREE FROM WHICH THEY HAVE FALLEN TO THANK IT FOR ITS BLESSING. Bless the acorns under a full moon, and recharge them every month. Give your partner one acorn to carry, and carry the other yourself. ★ MISTLETOE, OF COURSE, PRESIDES OVER YULETIDE KISSES, WONDERING WHOM TO FAVOR WITH ITS BLESSINGS OF FERTILITY. You could simply carry a piece while you're wishing to conceive. ★ TAKE AN OAK BATH (SEE PAGE 138) BEFORE MAKING LOVE WHEN YOU'RE TRYING TO CONCEIVE. ★ FINALLY, YOU CAN MAKE A FERTILITY ALTAR, DRESSED IN FRESH GREEN FLOWERS, AND WITH A GREEN CANDLE THAT YOU SHOULD BURN TO SEEK THE BLESSINGS OF NATURE. Pray each day to the female divinity, and ask to be allowed to share in the powers of creation.

Three for a girl ★ A SURE SPELL FOR A GIRL BABY. The desire to choose the sex of your child

is hardly new. The inheritance of the property and the power of the family often depended on giving birth to "heirs male," but daughters had their place, too. Not only important for ensuring marriage contracts (neighbors' conflicts were sorted out more easily through marriage than through war), daughters were a guarantee that any future offspring were unquestionably of your own family line. If, like me, you would love to have a daughter, or if there are already boys in the family and you're longing for a little balance, this spell will give you an excellent chance of having a girl. Of course, you have to begin before you're pregnant.

YOU WILL NEED

FOR EACH NIGHT: *3 pink dinner candles; lemon and lime essential oils; 3 flowers, preferably pinks; half a cup of freshly squeezed lemon juice; a douche*

★ BEFORE YOU BEGIN, YOU SHOULD SPEND AT LEAST A WEEK PRIOR TO OVULATION EATING A DIET OF ACID-RICH FOODS, OR, AT LEAST MAKE SURE THAT EVERY BREAKFAST IS FOLLOWED BY A GLASS OF ORANGE JUICE. It is helpful if your partner joins you in this. Work the ritual of this spell over three nights: your most fertile night and those on either side of it. On the evenings you have set aside, group the three candles closely together and light them, saying: *"The first candle was loneliness, / The second we both share, / The third is for our daughter, / For whom we now prepare."* Run yourself a warm but not hot bath to share with your partner, and add a capful of each essential oil. ★ AFTER A SHORT RELAXING BATH, PLACE THE THREE FLOWERS IN A VASE IN FRONT OF THE CANDLES, SAYING THE WORDS OF THE SPELL AGAIN BUT REPLACING THE WORD "CANDLE" WITH "FLOWER." While you do this, imagine a huge beam of pink-colored light circling through the room and cleansing the environment. ★ THE MOST IMPORTANT PART OF THE SPELL, PRIOR TO LOVEMAKING, IS THE DOUCHING. It is imperative that you douche with a solution of the lemon juice and one cup of warm water, and leave a little for your partner to bathe his vital parts in, too — this helps attract the egg. Let the juice take effect for about ten minutes, during which time you should both imagine the pink light surrounding you. *"Think Pink"* during your lovemaking, and let the candles burn down in the afterglow. ★ REPEAT THE SPELL ON THE FOLLOWING TWO NIGHTS.

Four for a boy ★

AN EQUALLY SURE SPELL FOR A BABY BOY. Not surprisingly perhaps, the more frequently used version of this spell was for a little boy, the time-honored guarantee of immortality for the family clan. This spell remained popular long after the heyday of other witchcraft—especially since in England and many other European countries, the inheritance of property and titles was dependent on producing a male heir. I hope, though, that this spell will be your choice only if you already have girls and want to bring a male balance to the family.

YOU WILL NEED

FOR EACH NIGHT: *4 blue dinner candles; dill seeds; 2 or 3 drops fennel oil; Epsom salts or baking soda; 4 blue periwinkles or bluebells (a fairy flower); a douche*

★ THIS SPELL FOLLOWS THE FORMAT OF THE SPELL FOR A GIRL, AND THE DIET PRIOR TO CONCEPTION IS JUST AS IMPORTANT BUT SHOULD BE ALKALINE RATHER THAN ACID. In days past this consisted mainly of a large consumption of soda bread (an Irish favorite) as well as adding dill seeds to salads and meat dishes, partly to counteract the acid reaction to food. Drinking fennel tea is helpful, and it goes without saying that the avoidance of acidic foods (like citrus fruits) is essential. ★ OVER THE THREE NIGHTS WHEN YOU HAVE CALCULATED YOUR OPTIMUM FERTILITY, LIGHT YOUR FOUR BLUE CANDLES IN THE BEDROOM, AT THE SAME TIME SAYING: *"One was lonely sorrow, / Two our coupled joy, / Three we have our little girl, / Four is for our boy."* Now you should run your bath with some fennel oil and either Epsom salts or, best of all, a large spoonful of baking soda. Take your bath together, relaxing and breathing in the fragrance. While you sit, cleanse the area around you from your mind with a beam of strong blue light, asking for a blessing on your magic. Retiring to the bedroom, group the candles near to the flowers, and caress each blue flower, at the same time saying the rhyme again. ★ SO MUCH FOR THE SPIRITUAL CONTENT OF YOUR SPELL. The vital physical piece is to douche with a mild solution of baking soda and warm water (about two teaspoons in half a cup of water) and, crucially, to ask your partner to sprinkle some baking soda on his organ (it doesn't sting). This is very important, so if he really wants a son, don't let him shrink (literally!) in embarrassment. Allow about ten minutes (no more) for the soda to work before lovemaking. ★ REPEAT THIS WHOLE RITUAL OVER THE FOLLOWING TWO NIGHTS.

Top 10 old wives' tales about pregnancy ★ "If it's

A GREAT YEAR FOR NUTS, IT'S A GREAT YEAR FOR CHILDREN." ★ CARRY A RABBIT'S FOOT FOR FERTILITY. ★ DON'T CROSS YOUR LEGS WHILE PREGNANT — it hinders birth. ★ DON'T GET MARRIED AFTER SUNSET IF YOU WANT TO BE SURE OF HAVING CHILDREN. ★ STREWING NUTS, ESPECIALLY HAZELNUTS, has the longest connection with fertility for young married couples. ★ IF YOU ARE IN THE COMPANY OF TWO PREGNANT WOMEN AND YOU WANT TO AVOID GETTING PREGNANT, slap your backside three times. ★ IF ANOTHER WOMAN'S BABY LOOKS RIGHT AT YOU FROM BETWEEN ITS LEGS, YOU WILL GET PREGNANT. ★ WEARING A COAT BELONGING TO OR SITTING IN A CHAIR OCCUPIED BY A PREGNANT WOMAN HAS THE SAME EFFECT. ★ IF A MOTHER GIVES AWAY ALL HER BABY CLOTHES AND THE CRADLE, she will be sure to have another baby (true in my case). ★ KISS UNDER THE MISTLETOE, THEN PICK ONE OF THE BERRIES, AND YOU WILL HAVE A CHILD WITHIN THE YEAR.

KEEP HIM HAPPY

The silken cord ★ Love entwined. This first spell has a long history; my grandmother used to describe it as "ancient," and seeing its classical symbolism I think it may have come to Britain with the Romans.

You will need

A strand of your loved one's hair and a strand of your own; some embroidery thread in three different colors of your own choice from the spectrum on page 11; 3 x 1 yard lengths of silken cord in colors to match the thread; some "Cupid's tears" oil: 2 or 3 drops each tuberose, jasmine, and ylang-ylang oils, and 1 drop musk oil, blended with ⅓ fluid ounce almond oil

★ Make a "girdle of Venus" from the ingredients, as follows. On the full moon, weave together the strands of your and your lover's hair, and wrap them in three colors of embroidery threads, securing all the ends into a knot. Now braid the cords, and as you work sing your love a song of love—any that makes you think of him or her by association. Weave the words of the song in with your girdle. In the center of the girdle, loop the hair and thread braid around the braided cords, then secure the ends with anything decorative you like: tassels are probably best, but you might choose charms or shells or anything that feels personal and satisfying. The girdle is complete, and you should wear it for the first time with the oil dabbed between breasts or behind knees or earlobes, etc., on a night that will undoubtedly witness unbridled passion. The magic of the girdle empowers the wearer, and the scents excite the nose that receives them.

My girlfriend Georgia wears her girdle to smart corporate dinners as well as for alfresco dinners in the garden. She seems to have Barry (her sexy but much older husband of many years) well and truly where she wants him—happy and mischievous with her alone.

The red ribbon ★ A SPELL FOR GIRLS TO DRIVE THEIR PARTNERS WILD.

YOU WILL NEED

1 yard of red ribbon; a few drops of "Cupid's tears" oil: 2 or 3 drops each tuberose, jasmine, and ylang-ylang oils, and 1 drop musk oil, blended with ⅓ fluid ounce almond oil; a beautiful hold-up stocking; tiny votive candles in rainbow colors to line the path to the bedroom

★ AFTER FIRST SPRINKLING THE RIBBON WITH A LITTLE OF THE OIL, TIE IT AROUND THE TOP OF YOUR STOCKINGED THIGH. Make the following incantation to Aphrodite: *"May I now recall the way I claimed my love's heart; / May I show him the palace of love incarnate; / Allow his cares to lighten and him to smilingly play his part. / So mote it be."* You must have the ribbon and stocking in place and seduce him with all your charms this night (no matter how hard his day at work or problems with partners and children and in-laws and automobiles). Light the way to the boudoir with the candles, and make this a romantic and passionate night to eclipse all others. ★ HEREAFTER, WHENEVER YOU CAN, PLACE THE RIBBON IN ODD PLACES FOR YOUR MAN TO FIND: in his organizer, his wallet, his briefcase, his pocket, around his teacup in the office (contrive this how you will). Each time he sees it, it will make him long to be with you.

My sexy friend Fiona sent a messenger to her man's car; using her spare key, the courier "broke in" and tied the ribbon around his steering wheel just before the end of the working day at his office. She also had the messenger tie the stocking around the gearshift, and I understand her man nearly drove off the road in his eagerness to get to her.

The magical note ★ MUSICIANS ARE REGARDED ASTROLOGICALLY AS THE "CHILDREN OF VENUS," AND SHAKESPEARE DESCRIBES MUSIC AS THE VERY "FOOD OF LOVE." Most of us have a song or piece that relates beyond anything else to the person we love. Music is fundamental to the workings of this next spell.

YOU WILL NEED

Some blank business cards, for your own special message; as many candles, votive size, as you have words in your song (see below); a few drops each of carnation, sandalwood, and frankincense oils; a musical note in the form of a charm, vase, or picture

★ FOR THIS SPELL, WHICH SENDS SIMPLE AND CLEAR MESSAGES OF LOVE MAGICALLY AND HYPNOTICALLY TO YOUR PARTNER, you need to settle on a few words of your own choice to pour into your lover's soul. Either choose some music that relates to your partner, such as a favorite song or piece you play or sing together, or speak from the heart and use your own imagination. In any case, choose words that are uplifting but unburdensome: *"I will always love you"* would be a good choice, but *"I can't live without you"* has connotations that are too heavy. ★ WRITE EACH WORD ON A CARD, and place each card under a votive candle. Blend the oils and anoint yourself and the candles. Hold the music charm in your hand, and sit in the center of the candles, thinking vividly of the sight, sound, and smell of your beloved. Breathe in his or her presence as if it were real. ★ NOW START THE MUSIC, AND LIGHT THE CANDLES IN THE SEQUENCE OF WORD ORDER. Imagine you are looking right into your loved one's eyes and dwell on some physical feature you like, such as a dimple, a curl, or a mole. Dwell on each and every word in turn, very slowly, one word at a time, as though you were trying to send just that word to your love's consciousness. Don't hurry. Smell the oils, which add concentration and clairvoyant ability, and continue to see the face, laugh, or smile that you love through each word transference. ★ MAINTAIN THE THOUGHTS LONG ENOUGH TO CONVEY THE WORDS OF THE WHOLE PHRASE, then imagine you are sending all the words and candlelight and smells through the air to your partner. Send laughter and a smile of your own by way of a "lots of love" at the end of your message; then release all together. Extinguish the candles one by one, and treasure the charm until you can give it to your love. You will shortly see a tangible sign of the spell's subconscious message at work. Your relationship will quite perceptibly become that little bit stronger.

Carnations, nuts, and ruby wine ★ To enhance a lackluster

SEXUAL RELATIONSHIP. It is crucial to perform a little magic ritual with the making of this brew. According to magic belief, the ritual and the words will transform the properties of the carnations that are at the center of this spell.

YOU WILL NEED

10 scented pinks (Dianthus caryophyllus); *a bottle of red wine; salad leaves; some whole nuts, including hazelnuts, walnuts, almonds, and pecans; oil and vinegar*

★ FIRST PERFORM YOUR COLOR-BREATHING RITUAL WITH LIGHTED CANDLES, then make a ring of the flowers and sit in their midst, facing east. Send a mental message to the one you love, whose physical presence you crave, and with whom you have a less than perfect sexual bond. Look in turn at every carnation flower and see your love's face therein. Inhale the perfume from each bloom, sending a mental message of its fragrance to your love. Breathe in the color and fragrance from the flowers, and then begin circling your head (very much as you would in a relaxation exercise) from the base of the neck. Be sure to work clockwise, for if you work "widdershins," or counterclockwise, your love affair will go backward and "unwind." Close your eyes and say: *"Scents and sense are for our ease; / Now our sensual love moves to a heightened phase."* ★ TAKE THE FLOWERS AND DENUDE THEM OF THEIR PETALS, BUT VERY LOVINGLY. Retain half in a plastic bag in the refrigerator for the salad, macerate the petals of the remaining flowers in the wine, then leave the mixture somewhere cool for eight days. Heat the liquid gently (never boil) and repeat the words over your "cauldron" (or whatever pot you are using to brew the wine). Strain and thus recover the ruby color of the wine; it should now be perfumed with the fragrant carnations. ★ ON THE NIGHT YOU WISH TO SIP THE BREW WITH YOUR BELOVED, make a green salad with any leaves you like, the nuts, and the petals of the remaining carnations. Dress lightly with oil and vinegar. (If you have time, add some clove carnations to the vinegar for a few days to intensify the flavor.) This should now form a first course, or with luck maybe the final course, of dinner. If your love affair had previously lacked a little lust, this should do the trick. Repeat whenever necessary.

Pasta lavandula ★

To calm the mind and excite the senses. This pasta dinner involves performing a spell before the arrival of the loved one, then throwing together a *diner à deux* based on lavender and its oil, which have the properties to soothe and calm while at the same time exciting the senses—ideal for preserving the perfect love. Quite literally, it injects the unexpected into the everyday.

You will need

6 x 1 yard lengths of lavender-colored ribbon, of varying lavender hues if desired; 1 bunch of lavender; 6 small lavender-scented candles; a small photo of you and your loved one together, smiling or laughing; ribbons of pasta prepared with a light dressing of olive oil, salt, and lavender flowers; a salad containing flowers

★ Begin by winding the six ribbons loosely around your right hand (or left, if you're left-handed), and keep them there while you work. ★ Place the bunch of lavender in a vase in the center of the table with a ring of candles around it, then set the table with the place settings opposite one another. ★ Pass the photograph across the lavender flowers in the table posy. Light the candles, pass the photograph over the flame of each one, then lay the photo in the middle of the ring of candles and imagine sending your partner a strong electric current of love in the shape of a beam of lavender-colored light. It will help you to do this if you touch the ribbons to the center of your forehead. Hold the vision of your loved one in the light for a few moments, then relax, unwind the ribbons from your hand, extinguish each candle gently, and encircle each candle with one of the ribbons. ★ Leave the table exactly like this while you prepare the dinner. Mix the lavender flowers, olive oil, and salt together and set aside. Prepare the salad. Cook the pasta and, just before you're ready to eat, add the lavender "pesto." Infuse all your love into the plate, and place it before your lover. Ask him or her to relight the candles (still with the ribbons encircling them) and wait to see what transpires at the end of the meal. **This spell is extremely effective if both partners are exhausted from everyday life and need help getting the romance and passion back into their relationship.**

The constellation ★ A SPELL TO PLACE YOUR LOVE AFFAIR IN THE HEAVENLY REALM.

You need to use your decorating skills to create your own beautiful firmament with deep blue background and golden stars forming a celestial canopy above the "marriage bed."

YOU WILL NEED

Some paint suitable for decorating the ceiling in evening-sky blue; some gold leaf, or good-quality gold paint; blue candles

★ THE BEAUTY OF THIS SYMBOLIC RITUAL IS TWOFOLD, in that you are creating a signature piece of artwork to bless your chamber, which should be aesthetically uplifting; and, when finished, you and your beloved will lie together under a microcosm of the heavens, in which your own individual beings are given special significance. The effect is to exalt your love. ★ SET TO WORK PAINTING THE SPACE ABOVE YOUR BED IN THE BLUE YOU FEEL HAPPY WITH. Take time and do not rush the job just to get it done, for the more effort you put into perfecting the decoration, the more you will be aware of the time it takes for a relationship to grow to full beauty. Once your backdrop is finished and dry, begin the magic of the task: Using your gold paint, create a galaxy of stars, the overall aim of which is to spell out subtly your and your love's initials, or names, or even symbols that act for each of you, by intertwining the stars across the night sky. Burn candles infused with incense or just of a solid color that suits your mood as you work. Pour love into your design, and think what concept of a divine love you can aspire to, and recognize. Play gentle music while you work if it pleases you. In short, use anything that helps to imbue the project with a peaceful, loving status under which your physical, earthly love can thrive. ★ REMEMBER THAT, AS WITH ALL MAGIC, this requires a level of mental focus and peaceful concentration; it is the thought forces that create the magic, and the physical work merely symbolizes your ideas, giving them a solid and tangible existence. ★ WHEN FIRST YOU LIE WITH YOUR PARTNER UNDER THIS CANOPY, preferably by candlelight, concentrate together on the effect of the "starlight," and make a pledge together to always seek to put your bond and life path onto the highest possible footing—walking in the stars.

MAKING UP

The ribbon of love 2 ★ Making contact.

This spell is intended for those who are waiting for the other side to make the approach after an argument. Use it if you're not sure where your lover is, or if you know he's just being reticent, or even as a preamble to making the telephone call yourself and being sure of a fair hearing. But beware: it won't work if you're the guilty party; having misbehaved or thrown a tantrum, you owe your partner an apology.

You will need

1 yard of red ribbon

★ Perform this spell on any moon or day of the week, but if the quarrel has been fierce and you need extra strength, use the full moon. You must also bring a calm mind to the task, since tearful outbursts and hot emotion will send confused signals to your partner and could cause fears of renewed hostility. ★ Wrap the ribbon around the index finger of your right hand and place it on your "third eye" (between your eyebrows). Start thinking intently of your loved one; when you have a clear and powerful sense of his closeness, use the ribbon on your forehead to "talk" to him and tell him you're sorry about the upset and would love to speak to him. Urge him to contact you. ★ Try to hold this concentration for a few minutes without letting your mind wander, then rest, sending him loving thoughts before you break off. Pick up the ribbon again in an hour and repeat the process, several times in the day/evening, if possible. He will soon be straining to contact you; when the call comes, don't be distant. Remember to meet him halfway.

Three candles bright ★ THE IDEAL CHOICE IF A THIRD PARTY IS CAUSING TROUBLE

BETWEEN YOU AND YOUR LOVED ONE. This need not necessarily be a past lover, but perhaps an over-possessive child from a previous relationship, or an in-law (my husband calls them "outlaws").

YOU WILL NEED

3 candles, colors chosen from the rainbow spectrum to represent the 3 different parties (such as birthday number or star-sign colors [see pages 151–152])

★ NOTCH THE CANDLES IN SIX EQUAL PLACES (TO BURN THE CANDLES DOWN OVER SIX NIGHTS). WHEN THEY ARE ALIGHT, say aloud the name of your "adversary," adding: *"Let go your immaturity and fear, / Let (name of the loved one) find love's security right here."* Touch your heart as you say this, and wish the other person well. Repeat this over the next five days, and you will find his or her possessiveness gradually lessens.

The beech leaf spell ★ IF BOTH YOU AND YOUR LOVED ONE HAVE BEEN BRUISED IN

LOVE TOO OFTEN, perform this spell at the first sign of difficulty between you.

YOU WILL NEED

A beech leaf, picked on a warm day; a book of value, such as a missal, diary, or volume of love poetry

★ HOLD THE BEECH LEAF TO YOUR HEART AND ASK THAT IT CLEANSE YOU AND GIVE YOU NEW SPIRIT. Taking it from your heart, secretly stroke it over your love's brow (contrive a little tickle or gesture of affection), silently urging it to cleanse away negativity and fear. Smile at your love, then place the leaf reverently into the chosen book. Sleep on this for a month, and the love between you will wax. (This spell also works well if you have been having trouble deciding that a past love affair is truly over.)

Frozen honey ★ To sweeten him or her up. This is another excellent spell for improving relations after a fight. It is also a good choice if relations have been souring between you for a little while and you want to sweeten things up.

You will need

For the cleansing bath: *Salt; valerian root; rosemary; and rue (though be careful with this last if you have sensitive skin, as you may react to the contact—handle it on a cloudy day); rose oil*

For the spell: *2 small pieces of paper with your and your partner's names written, one on each; a tiny plastic pot or container; some vervain leaves; a small pot of clover honey; a freezer*

★ If you really want to put your heart and soul into this spell, you should begin by running yourself a cleansing bath before you do it. This is a warm bath to which is added a spoonful of salt, along with some crushed valerian root, rosemary, and rue. Take your thoughts of love with you into the bath, and, with an honest heart, speak out loud your reasons for choosing to perform the honey spell. Make sure you are really motivated by love and not by a wish to bind your love to you. After your bath, rub your hands with a little lotion to which you have added a few drops of rose oil. ★ Now you are ready to perform the spell: Place the two pieces of paper, on which your names are written, together so that the names face in to each other, and place them at the bottom of your container. Put a few vervain leaves on top. Now take the honey and pour it into the container so that it generously covers the contents. Make a vow of warmth and affection to your love, and say: *"Sweeten ye up, in this healing cup."* Pass your hands over the top three times in a caressing gesture, then imagine a honey-colored glow bathing you and your love as you stand together, holding hands. Finally, place the container in a space in your freezer where it will not be disturbed. ★ Within a few days you should detect a definite improvement in the relationship.

Honeyed rose ★ THIS IS A BEAUTIFUL EMBODIMENT OF ENTWINED LOVE, which has the added

bonus of resolving quarrels and past strife.

YOU WILL NEED

2 pieces of paper about 3 x 1¼ inches; a tiny jar; some honey; a beautiful rose bush, traditionally a two-colored variety such as R. 'Chicago Peace' or R. 'Granada'

★ WRITE YOUR NAME ON ONE OF THE TWO PIECES OF PAPER AND YOUR PARTNER'S ON THE OTHER, KISS THEM, AND TIE THEM INTO A KNOT TOGETHER. Put them together in the little jar, cover them with honey, then replace the lid. Now, plant your rose, with your partner's help if possible, but alone if circumstances so dictate. Say something like: *"We are earthly creatures, living here on this earth, which is sweetened by the gifts of nature's bounty and by the knowledge for each of us of the other's existence. May we make of our earthly selves the most that we can, and joining together, sweeten and beautify our own and our friends' existences."* Water, cherish, and love your rose. Cut blooms from it regularly to place at your love altar. Every year, place a new "knot" in the soil under its roots, and restate your love and intent.

A loving cup ★ MAKE THIS LOVE POTION TO SIP WITH YOUR PARTNER AT YOUR FIRST MEETING

TOGETHER AFTER A RIFT. Blend your brew in advance, and allow it to steep for several days in a cool closet.

YOU WILL NEED

1 teaspoon apothecary's rose petals; a few leaves of costmary; a pinch of saffron; a bottle of sherry

★ CRUSH THE HERBS AND FLOWERS TOGETHER (THE COSTMARY INTENSIFIES THE SCENT OF THE ROSES AND SAFFRON) AND ADD TO THE BOTTLE OF SHERRY. Store in a cool place for a few days. When you wish to serve it to your partner, strain into small glasses. This lovely concoction will ease the tensions at what otherwise might be a tricky meeting.

The candle of truth ★ To know if someone is deceiving you. Sometimes you may

feel you can put the past behind you only if you know the absolute truth about what has happened to cause the rift; then you can forgive and heal. Be sure you really want to know what your loved one has to say before you do this, the truth spell.

You will need

A mirror; a white candle; incense of narcissus oil to relax your partner; a vase of geraniums or primroses; a glass of wine

★ This spell should be performed only on the 7th of the month. Invite your love to sit in front of a mirror with the offer of a neck and shoulder massage. In front of you light the white candle and burn the oil—very relaxing. You should also have the flowers, all symbols of doubt until better acquainted, in front of the mirror. ★ As you work your hands, speak softly and hypnotically so your love relaxes completely. When you feel the moment is right, ask three questions. Ask the reflection of your lover's face and make sure he answers the reflection of yours. The first two questions should not be too serious—rather lighthearted, in fact. They could relate to your love's plans for the week at work or be about his family. Notice his expression as he answers. Finally, ask him the question to which you want to know the truthful answer. If he answers honestly, you will know from his face in the mirror—for, though he may be able to fib a little to others, he cannot lie to himself. You will know!

FAMILY MATTERS

Protection spells ★

TWO TREES, SACRED TO THE DRUIDS, HAVE LONG BEEN WELL KNOWN FOR THEIR PROTECTIVE POWERS. In fact, the expression "knock on wood," to make sure your luck holds, comes from the practice of touching trees to secure the blessing of the tree spirits, which later was replaced by the idea of touching a piece of Christ's true cross. ★ IF YOU WANT TO GIVE YOUR FAMILY AND HOME EXTRA HELP AND PROTECTION, THE FIRST STEP WOULD BE TO PLANT A ROWAN TREE, OR MOUNTAIN ASH—for it is asserted that anyone dwelling in a house hosting this tree shall be blessed and have special protection from fairy and angel folk. ★ THE SECOND TREE OF PROTECTION AND, SOME SAY, ONE WITH THE POWER TO GRANT WISHES, IS THE WITCHES' FAVORITE, THE WILLOW. This was one of the original Druid trees from the tree/moon calendar (see page 153), and the moon associated with it is sometimes called "Willow moon, the witches' moon." The willow has powers of love, healing, and fertility, but if you want particularly to safeguard your home, family, and property, grow a willow in the garden near a stream or old well to influence the Fates.

A willow spell ★

TO PROTECT THE FAMILY. If you're a city dweller who wishes to protect your home and family, you can bring willow branches into your house or apartment and make a kind of altar for them. You can also do the following spell.

YOU WILL NEED

2 drops each rosemary, geranium, and frankincense oils in about ½ fluid ounce almond oil; willow branches for cleansing; a growing cyclamen plant; a white candle

★ CHOOSE A WAXING MOON. Burn the oils in a burner, and carry it through the rooms of your home to cleanse them all. In the area of the hearth or wherever you all sit grouped most often, perform your spell. Lay the willow branches and the potted cyclamen (white or red is best) on a table, and light a pure white candle. With your herb oils still burning and with vivid thought, take a beam of white light from the candle in your mind's eye and spin it like a tornado around the room and around each member of the household, cleansing away all negativity. Each morning you can surround your family afresh with this protective white light. ★ TAKE THE WILLOW BRANCHES AND WEAVE THEM INTO A SMALL WREATH, bathe it in the white light, and hang it above your front door. Light a fresh white candle in the same place once a month on the new moon to recharge the positive atmosphere.

"Child in honey, child in light" ★ To control a stubborn child.

All the psychological strategies you can think of are often powerless against the wiles of a willful child. They seem to embarrass us effortlessly at social occasions and sometimes prove a danger to themselves, too, as they career toward some impending catastrophe.

You will need

A small photo of your child; a jar of lavender or clover honey; sealing wax; 1 yard of white ribbon

★ PERFORM THIS SPELL ON A THURSDAY, WITH A WAXING MOON. Before you begin, spend a few minutes in your child's room, soaking up the feeling of the child; breathe in their smell and their aura, and imagine you can hear their laughter. Take the best element of your child's behavior with you in your mind, and go to your protection altar to make your spell. All the while you are working, think of your child cocooned in a spiral of white light. ★ PLACE THE SMALL PHOTO INSIDE THE JAR OF HONEY, SAYING: *"Child in honey, child in light, / Let your cares take elfin flight; / Smooth your thorns, be gone sour moods, / And witness sunshine interludes. / Stamp your foot no more from hence, / Nor show you such indifference. / Speech is silver, silence gold—Now you must do just as you're told! / With love."* ★ SEND ALL YOUR LOVE TO YOUR CHILD, AND RESEAL THE JAR. Add sealing wax around the rim, and secure with a white ribbon. Place the jar on a high shelf or cabinet, out of the way but not somewhere dark. ★ EVERY SO OFTEN, TOUCH THE JAR AND REPEAT THE WORDS TO RECHARGE THE POWER OF THE SPELL.

To end conflict between siblings ★ HERE IS ANOTHER SPELL TO

HELP WITH FRACTIOUS CHILDREN, THIS TIME BROTHERS AND/OR SISTERS WHO FIGHT. Get your children to do the spell above with a photo of each other, both placed in the honey jar together, telling them it will bring them good luck and grant a wish if they kiss afterward and are good. You must say the incantation, but having them do the action is very effective.

Cutting the cord ★ To make overprotective parents loosen their grip. This procedure

encourages your family to hold on to you less tightly, without losing the bond of warmth.

You will need

1 yard of red cord or ribbon; a photo of your parents; a pair of pinking shears tied with a white bow

★ Working on a waning moon, take your cord or ribbon and bind it around the index finger of your right hand. Place it to your "third eye" (between your eyebrows) and close your eyes, thinking lovingly of your parents. Take the photo of them and hold it in front of you, looking deeply at the image, while you send a strong mental message to them to loosen their hold on you without fear of losing your love. Now take the ribbon and cut it in half with the bow-tied shears; kiss both halves and keep them in separate drawers. ★ Send them a blessing for their safety, and ask them to relax. You should notice an immediate difference.

A rosemary remedy ★ To help restore your concentration. There are times when

none of the family are quite performing at their peak. Tension, stress, or overtiredness can all be contributing to a general sense of malaise, so here is an excellent ritual to help get your concentration and mental energy back on track. You will find over the years it has many applications.

You will need

½ cup freshly picked rosemary; rosemary oil; a base lotion or thick, good-quality night cream, preferably unperfumed

★ This draws on rosemary's ancient association with waking up the brain, an association so strong that ancient Greek scholars wore garlands of the herb to help them think. ★ If someone in the family is preparing for an exam or studying hard, prepare a tea of rosemary using flowering tops, or several sprigs if the flowers are not out, and infusing in one quart of boiling water. Leave it for five to ten minutes, strain, and have them drink three cupfuls through the day, sweetening it with honey if desired. Before they go into their exam (or meeting), rub a mild ointment of rosemary on their temples: about two drops of rosemary oil mixed with one tablespoon of good-quality skin lotion. This will stimulate their senses and keep them alert. This could make all the difference.

To calm a relative or friend in distress ★ THERE COMES

A TIME IF A CLOSE FRIEND OR RELATIVE IS IN SEVERE DISTRESS, WHEN TEA AND SYMPATHY ARE NOT QUITE ENOUGH AND YOU REALLY NEED TO TAKE CONTROL OF A SPIRALING SITUATION. Whether the crisis has occurred through some shock to the system (such as witnessing an accident) or perhaps with the breakup of a relationship or even the loss of a pet, the following spell will help to soothe savaged nerves.

YOU WILL NEED

Bach Rescue Remedy (available from most health food stores); frankincense oil; light tea made from rose hip or, better still, apothecary's rose petals (a handful of dried petals to 1 quart boiling water, brewed for 10 minutes); an unperfumed hand cream; 2 drops rose oil

★ THE FIRST THING YOU MUST DO TO CALM SOMEONE WHO IS HIGHLY NERVOUS IS TO MAKE THEM FEEL SECURE BUT NOT DETAINED: HAVE THEM SIT IN A SUPPORTIVE, ENVELOPING CHAIR, BUT GIVE THEM ROOM TO BREATHE. Your own movements must be as calm as possible and your voice hypnotically low and soothing. As soon as possible, drip two or three drops of Bach Rescue Remedy on their tongue, then light the frankincense oil and brew the tea. While you are waiting for it to steep, mix the hand cream with the rose oil and rub it very gently but firmly into the invalid's hands, massaging particularly at the wishbone joint between the thumb and index finger. Work continually, but don't appear hurried: your own calm, airy lightness of being will have a direct impact on the nerves of the patient. ★ SERVE THE TEA (ADD HONEY IF NEED BE, AS SWEETNESS WILL HELP THE SHOCK), THEN START LAYING YOUR HANDS ON THEM: FIRST ON THEIR TEMPLES, THEN ON THEIR NECK, SHOULDERS, AND ARMS. In each resting place, use all your mind power to inject gentle heat and light from your inner being into your friend. Imagine the light going right through their confused body, penetrating from each entry zone you touch. Do this for about ten minutes, while they sip at the tea. This is also a very good general tonic for older people and convalescents. When you have finished, wind the energy force down in your mind and imagine a very comforting hand slowly stroking their whole body. By all means actually do this if you feel you can. Finally, just lay your right hand on their right lower arm; you should be able to feel your hand tingling slightly. If they now feel exhausted, encourage them to rest without moving too far. They will rouse themselves later feeling much more relaxed. ★ DO THIS SEVERAL TIMES OVER A WEEK IF THE CONDITIONS INDICATE THAT IT WOULD BE BENEFICIAL.

Pet hypnosis ★ How to deal with a psychotic pet. Pets are by no means the least important

family members, and they should not be left out of the playful side of our magic. My daughter's pet rabbit behaves like a cat, lying on its back with paws in the air in front of the fire; a friend's budgerigar barks at their dog; and one of my neighbors has a huge Old English sheepdog which is terrified of small dogs! So what can you do if your white cat wishes he were black? If your pet has a nervous disposition which is spoiling their life or yours, try the next spell to uncross their hooves or unruffle their whiskers.

YOU WILL NEED

Essential oils: melissa (lemon balm) if your pet is highly strung, clary sage if it is aggressive or hostile,
bergamot if it seems despondent or depressed; a blue candle; catnip (½ cup dried leaves or flowering tops);
classical music (Mozart and Monteverdi recommended)

★ First you must cleanse the animal's sleeping quarters by sending white light in a strong beam from your mind's eye around the whole area. Next, take the chosen essential oil(s) and sprinkle a couple of drops on their rug or cushion or whatever they sleep on. Pets have very sensitive noses and will sneeze if the dose is too direct or too strong. Burn a blue candle where your pet will look at the flame from time to time (it shouldn't be difficult to make them curious about what you're doing), and say a chant to both candle and pet, in which you repeat your pet's name three times followed by *"calm calm calm"* several times. ★ Give your pet a few chopped-up catnip leaves (no problem for cats, rabbits, hamsters, mice etc.; for a dog, make a light tea and cool it right down, giving just a small amount as a drink). Catnip, apart from its notoriously aphrodisiac reputation for cats, is good for soothing fevers and has mild sedative properties which are effective and safe even for children. Finally, hold a music appreciation class for at least an hour a day for your pet: play some classical music very softly for them. This has more than a calming effect—some people say it improves the milk yield of cows and goats, and its effects on plants have been much discussed. Keep up this course of action over a week or so, and spend a certain amount of time stroking and playing with the animal beforehand. ★ Because animals are so very sensitive, you may get results faster with them than with any other family member.

MIRROR, MIRROR

All dolled up ★ A witch's potion to help shed pounds.

You will need

3 tablespoons fennel seeds; a "poppet" (a doll to represent a person); patchouli oil; fennel oil (optional)

★ As you are trying to rid yourself of extra weight, work on a waning moon: many women begin diets on waxing moons and can't understand why they can't stay with them. Make up a pot of fennel tea by steeping the seeds in a pint of boiling water for five minutes, then drink it during the day. This age-old remedy is known to speed up the digestion of fatty foods and help sluggishness and flatulence. Taken in conjunction with a sensible eating regime it could make all the difference to staying with, and benefiting from, a slimming diet. Your doll is supposed to represent you. It could be bought or homemade, and you should dress it in clothes that represent you. It should start off swathed in layers of clothes; then each week, you remove an outer layer. This ritual is very important, as it helps to channel your belief in yourself, and see yourself actually as a person of decreasing size. ★

The patchouli oil can be burned during the day, but is even more effective massaged into the body (always dilute in a base oil: a few drops of essence to $\frac{1}{3}$ fluid ounce almond oil). You could also add a few drops of fennel oil. When you have achieved your ideal size, place your slimmer doll in a key position in the kitchen, and reduce your intake of fennel tea to one cup a day.

To charm away warts ★ There must be more than a thousand variations of

wart-charming spells, but this one I have found to be reliable and easy to perform!

You will need

A silver dish or bowl; some dandelions; lemon essential oil

★ Since you are driving the wart away, perform this spell on a waning moon. By moonlight, bathe the affected area in a silver dish half-filled with water into which you have placed some dandelions. Say these words: "*By the moon's eternal light, / Drive away this ugly sight.*" Rub the dandelions onto the wart to release the sap, and pat dry. It is traditional to bury the herbs, which you can do if you wish; otherwise just discard them. Last thing at night, dab some undiluted lemon oil onto the wart area. By morning you will see an improvement. You should continue the use of the dandelions and the oil for the remainder of the waning moon. ★ The sap from the dandelion has a proven effect on warts.

Crowning glory ★

A SEDUCTIVE HAIR RINSE TO ATTRACT ATTENTION. The Irish, too, have some wise words on the subject of love. This hair tonic, which comes from Ireland and was conceived in the days before designer shampoos, makes your hair gleam and bewitches everyone with the intoxicating smell of your tresses.

YOU WILL NEED

1 tablespoon orrisroot; ½ cup finely chopped parsley; ½ cup macerated lavender flowers

★ AFTER SHAMPOOING YOUR HAIR BEFORE A PARTY OR A DATE, STIR THE INGREDIENTS INTO A CUP OF WARM SPRING WATER TO MAKE A RINSE. Let it steep for half an hour and use after or in place of conditioner. You will be delighted with the effects as you attract attention like bees to nectar!

Wreathed in smiles ★

TO BRING SUNSHINE INTO YOUR LIFE. Another beautiful spell for the hair can be worked at the height of summer, when glorious sunflowers are in full bloom. If you can put aside an hour on a sunny Sunday, this spell is ideal for a daytime date.

YOU WILL NEED

A few drops of sunflower oil; 7 sunflowers; 1 yard of yellow ribbon

★ BEFORE GOING OUT TO A DAYTIME OCCASION, MASSAGE A FEW DROPS OF SUNFLOWER OIL INTO YOUR SCALP AND THE ENDS OF YOUR HAIR. Make a circle on the ground with the sunflowers and lie with your hair inside the circle in the full sunshine. Chant to the Archangel Michael, or Helios, to send down a love for you during the sunlight hours, which come under his dominion, then close your eyes and try to see through the light of your lashes the face of the one who will be yours. Sit up, wind the yellow ribbon around your right forefinger, place it to your "third eye" (between your eyebrows), and ask again for a new love to bring sunshine into your life. Concentrate for a few minutes, then unwind the ribbon. ★ WASH THE OIL OUT OF YOUR HAIR, TIE THE YELLOW RIBBON AROUND YOUR HEAD, AND SECURE THE FLOWERS BENEATH THE BAND TO MAKE A FLOWERY HEADDRESS. Say out loud the names of the seven days of the week, and wear the wreath on your date.

★ WITHIN THE WEEK, YOU SHOULD HAVE MET SOMEONE WITH A SUNNY PERSONALITY.

To cure a minor illness ★ A RITUAL FOR PICKING AND CHARGING VERVAIN.

This holy herb was renowned for centuries for its medicinal value and its magical properties. The Druids prized it as highly as their beloved mistletoe, and legend told that it was found on Mount Calvary and used to stanch Christ's wounds. ★ VERVAIN HAS BEEN USED OVER THE YEARS TO KEEP EVIL SPIRITS FROM THE HOUSE. IT HAS BEEN MIXED IN LOVE POTIONS AND DRUNK AS A TEA FOR A HUNDRED COMPLAINTS. It is very refreshing if brewed in boiling water and then added to bathwater. Use it as your intuition dictates, and whenever you gather it, say these enchanter's words: *"Oh healing hand, thou holy herb, Vervain, / Which groweth here upon the ground, / Blessed be the field or lane, / Where'er your leaf is found."* ★ You will find that ½ cup dried leaves steeped in a pint of boiling water relieves indigestion and upset stomachs; twice this strength is used to treat a cut or wound or burn and can be gargled for throat problems and mouth ulcers.

Lavender and basil ★ TO CURE A HEADACHE. Lavender is well known for its relaxing

properties, which may explain why it can help to cure tension headaches.

YOU WILL NEED

A sachet of dried lavender or a compress dipped in lavender oil; 1 yard of green ribbon; a basil leaf

★ SMELL THE LAVENDER AND BREATHE ITS FRAGRANCE RIGHT INTO YOUR SYSTEM TO CLEANSE AND RELAX YOURSELF (OR YOU CAN PLACE THE COMPRESS ON YOUR HEAD FOR A FEW MINUTES). Take your ribbon and wind it around the index finger of your left hand. Place it to your "third eye" (between your eyebrows), and gently rub back and forth over it. Now unwind the ribbon and wrap it around your forehead like a headband, securing a basil leaf under it over the third eye. Relax for ten minutes completely, and imagine the poisons draining out of your forehead into the ribbon. When you feel a lightening of the ache, remove the ribbon, cut it in half and discard it. This should lessen even a violent headache and drive off a persistent one.

To cure a cold ★

THERE MUST BE AS MANY RECIPES FOR CURING THE COMMON COLD AS THERE ARE WART INCANTATIONS, because until relatively recently, a chill could be life threatening. I've found the following remedy to be effective.

YOU WILL NEED

1 pound fresh onions; gingerroot; garlic; elderflowers (fresh, if possible; otherwise a good commercial elderflower tea); honey if desired or if you have a cough as well; 2 teaspoons dry mustard powder; ginger and eucalyptus essential oils

★ TO HAVE THE BEST SUCCESS WITH THIS REMEDY, YOU SHOULD BEGIN AS SOON AS YOU RECOGNIZE COLD SYMPTOMS STARTING; IN FACT, IF YOU GET IT EARLY ENOUGH, YOU CAN PREVENT THE ONSET ALTOGETHER. Take one onion and quarter it, then place one quarter in each corner of your house to begin the battle against the spread of the infection. With the remaining onions make a French onion soup (don't take a shortcut and use packet mixes), which you will sup on through the course of a few days. While your soup is cooking, make your herb tonic: Grate some fresh gingerroot and put it with some crushed garlic into a mug; add the elderflowers (or elder tea), and steep for ten minutes before drinking. Add honey, if necessary. ★ MEANWHILE, MAKE A HOT FOOTBATH BY ADDING THE DRY MUSTARD POWDER TO HOT WATER IN A BASIN, AND SOAK YOUR FEET WHILE YOU SIP YOUR TEA. Sit somewhere comfortable and relax. Experience the wonderful warmth spreading from your feet, slowly up through your whole body, relaxing it, casting away tension, and driving off the malady. Over a ten-minute period, try to feel your whole body glowing with warmth and triumphing over infection. ★ DRINK YOUR TEA AND SOAK YOUR FEET THIS WAY TWO OR THREE TIMES IN THE DAY; FOLLOW WITH A LIGHT MEAL OF THE ONION SOUP. Wage this war for up to three days, and you should be the victor. During this period, burn the oils in the house; they will neutralize the sickness, and you will absorb their healing essences.

Top 10 witch's beauty tips ★

THE METEORIC RISE IN POPULARITY OF HERBAL POTIONS AND ESSENTIAL OILS CAN BE ATTESTED BY THE VARIETY OF PRODUCTS NOW ON THE MARKET. In almost any good-sized town, there is now someone specializing in selling flower- or herb-based lotions for skin, hair, nails, and all varieties of cosmetic use. *Here is a more traditional selection of witchy tips.* ★ TO STAY YOUTHFUL: Macerate about a handful of the flowering tips and leaves of rosemary and marjoram in 1¼ cups alcohol for a month; add honey and two tablespoons of fresh blackcurrant juice; strain through a fine sieve, and take half a teaspoon two or three times a week. It also eases aches, strains, and pains, and even helps with rheumatic disorders. ★ TO IMPROVE THE TEXTURE OF THE SKIN AND SOOTHE RASHES: Place the leaves and flowers of a handful of St. Johnswort in a glass jar, just cover with olive or almond oil, let stand for a month, strain, and use as a compress to treat rashes and inflammations. Some people develop a light sensitivity with this herb, so it is very important to remember not to go out in the sun directly after you have used it. ★ TO TREAT BURNS, SCALDS, SNAKE BITES, AND PIMPLES: Macerate ½ cup fresh lavender flowers in 2½ cups olive oil in the sunlight for three days, strain through a fine sieve or muslin, and repeat the procedure for three more days. The highly perfumed oil should be stored in a dark glass bottle in a cool place and can be applied in small quantities as needed. ★ TO LIGHTEN FRECKLES: Crush some orrisroot to extract the juice and add to the bruised leaves of watercress; apply a small amount of the resulting liquid with a cotton swab. ★ TO AID IN THE ELIMINATION OF CELLULITE: Make a tea from ½ cup meadowsweet flowers infused for ten minutes in 2½ cups not-quite-boiling water. Drink two cups of tea a day. Accompany this with massage of the affected areas using ⅓ fluid ounce almond oil, four drops of cypress oil, and two drops of lemon essential oil. Treat for one month. ★ TO IMPROVE THE APPEARANCE OF DULL SKIN: Finely grind the flowering tops of evening primrose flowers, add to a paste made of almond oil and ground almonds, then apply as a face mask for ten minutes. This gives the skin a lovely radiance. ★ TO REDUCE HAIR LOSS: Prepare a tonic of 1 cup nasturtium leaves, seeds, and flowers, ½ cup nettle leaves, two tablespoons of marigold flowers, two tablespoons of lavender flowers, four sprigs of rosemary, and a handful of oak leaves, all macerated for a month in 2½ cups alcohol. Sieve three times, and use twice a week as a pre-shampoo treatment, leaving it on for at least 20 minutes. ★ TO IMPROVE THE CONDITION OF NAILS AND HAIR: Make a solution of lavender by steeping ten flowering sprigs in 2½ cups nearly-boiling water for 30 minutes. Add one tablespoon of the resulting tonic to the pressed juice of watercress *(Nasturtium officinale)*, and apply to the scalp and hair after shampooing and conditioning to strengthen and thicken it. Add a few drops to a hand cream and rub into the nails. Eat plenty of watercress and evening primrose (either in capsule form or by adding the flowers to salads) to increase the effect internally.

THE WILL TO SUCCEED

Money to burn ★ A candle spell to get your finances moving.

You will need

Hyssop oil; a bunch of daisies; a green cloth; 1 yard of red ribbon; a green dinner candle;
a bank note in any currency, worth about $1

★ Work this spell on a waxing moon, preferably on a Thursday or, to influence a specific contract or to aid in buying property, on a Saturday. First prepare your altar by burning some hyssop essential oil and placing some freshly cut daisies on a green cloth. Wind the red cord around the middle finger of your right hand and place on your breast. Concentrate all your force on attracting a busy, prosperous earning period ahead and also, if you wish, on the possibility of gaining a bonus, such as a windfall or an unexpected lump sum; but do not allow greed to turn your head. Take the green candle and anoint it with hyssop oil, then light the candle with the money, and say: *"Within one week, / Those things we seek, / Will come within our power; / All worries go, / And money flow, / In plenty from this hour."* ★ Ask your partner (in business or love) to repeat the verse with you a second time if you want to attract good luck as a pair. Let the candle burn down safely during the course of the day. Keep just the stub (no more than 1 inch) tied with the red ribbon in a bow for a week after the spell, somewhere near or on the altar with the flowers. ★ Within the week, you should experience some particularly uplifting signs in business that you didn't anticipate; or, if you are awaiting the outcome of a job interview, you should get the answer you want.

A variation on this spell can be done specifically on the eve of an important business venture or the launch of a project. Write the name of your company and/or partners or just a short description of the business plan you are unfolding on a piece of green paper. Add a drop or two of hyssop oil to it, then wrap it up inside the money and continue in the same way, burning names and cash together as you light the candle. At the end of the ritual, when you are tying the ribbon around the candle stump, write again the name of your venture or partners, and attach them to the candle inside the ribbon. Keep this safe in a small pouch until the venture has succeeded.

Hot wax ★

A RITUAL TO ENSURE YOUR BEST CHANCE OF SUCCESS BEFORE A PRIZE DRAWING. If you are hoping to win a bonus of money in a prize drawing, sweepstakes, or lottery, here is a spell you can do to improve your chances; but remember that balance is part of the creed of magic, *and greed is not!* If you have a good purpose in mind, and plan to distribute some of your winnings in one or two other charitable directions, you may meet with more success than someone who is motivated by pure selfishness. Remember, too, that scale is relative; you will be considered lucky to win $500, despite the fact that you might wish to make the sum ten times greater.

YOU WILL NEED

Peony, hyssop, or frankincense oils; a red or gold dinner candle; a pin or sharp-pointed pen; a gold cord

★ THIS SPELL MUST BE PERFORMED ON A WAXING MOON. If you were to do the spell on a waning moon, the opposite might happen, and you might find yourself instead the recipient of masses of mysterious bills! Before you begin the spell, you should burn some prosperity-related oil or scent to attract finances to your home: peony is the best for this, but hyssop and frankincense are also good. If you are inspired by Asian ideology, make almond essence your choice. ★ TAKE YOUR CANDLE AND WARM IT FIRST, EITHER OVER ANOTHER CANDLE'S FLAME OR ON A WARM SURFACE, SO THAT THE WAX DOWN ONE EDGE IS SOFT AND PLIABLE. Take your sharp implement and write your name in flowing script down the soft edge of the candle. Light the candle and see the bright glow of success and delight in its flame; imagine that you are surprised by winning a prize or cash bonus. As you watch the flame burn down, make a pledge about what you would do if favored with lucky money, and make only promises you know you would keep; *please don't be greedy and think of large sums.* During the ceremony, rise and make your pledge also to the moon, and do not specify a date or time by which you ask to be favored. After the candle has burned down to the stump, extinguish it and take it with you, tied with gold cord, to buy your ticket or enter your draw. ★ IF YOUR PLEDGE HAS BEEN SEEN AS SINCERE, YOU MAY MEET WITH EXTRAORDINARY GOOD FORTUNE.

Many people prefer to do this spell in stages, burning the candle three times, to equal notches, over the course of the waxing moon, until the day just before full. This means you might be preparing for luck at any stage, and your chances will be even stronger.

Busy as a bee ★

A SPELL TO BRING IN MORE WORK. This spell must be the automatic choice if you're usually inundated with work but, for some reason, things have recently gone a little flat and you're not as busy as you'd like to be. This is like a secret telegraph wire that sends your full-page advertisement into the ether.

YOU WILL NEED

Your business card; a pen; a bag of absorbent cotton in one piece; a 12-inch length of red ribbon; a small frosted glass bottle with stopper; a jar of honey; a baby oak tree (optional)

★ FOR THIS SPELL TO WORK BEST YOU SHOULD CHOOSE A WAXING MOON, PREFERABLY A BRAND-NEW ONE. Sit calmly, with your ingredients in front of you, and strongly visualize your happiest moments of industry. See yourself busy with a challenging workload and any others around you also cheerfully employed with work they're happy to do. Consider briefly whether, in the past, you've sometimes been so bent on meeting deadlines that you've been unable to eat properly or complained that there simply weren't enough hours in the day. Make a mental note to correct this imbalance, to make time for those who are important to you, and never again to complain about having too much to do. Say out loud, *"My life and accounts shall soon be in balance,"* and pick up your business card. Use the pen to draw on the back of the card a simple picture of a busy bee, buzzing from flower to flower. Imagine yourself in the same role, happy in your work. ★ LAY THE CARD ON A PIECE OF ABSORBENT COTTON, AND ROLL BOTH INTO A SMALL, CYLINDRICAL SHAPE, REPEATING THE WORDS ABOVE AS YOU DO THIS. Using the red ribbon, tie the little scroll up with a small neat bow and "mail" it through the mouth of the bottle, then fill it to the brim with honey. Place the stopper in the top, repeating the words above. If you live in the country or have a garden, you should now dig a hole to plant a baby oak tree, putting the bottle underneath and saying: *"My life and accounts shall soon be in balance, and my house and happiness shall flourish."* If you cannot plant a tree, or live in an apartment in town, say the same words while placing the bottle in your freezer. Every evening while the moon is still waxing, either water your oak or turn your bottle clockwise in the freezer, repeating the words as you do this. ★ DON'T LET YOUR TREE GO THIRSTY OR YOUR FREEZER DEFROST, AND BY THE NEXT NEW MOON, THINGS SHOULD HAVE PICKED UP CONSIDERABLY.

"Sugar and spice and everything nice" ★ To attract

A SHOWER OF GIFTS. This spell is for those who would love to be given items of value by their lovers; but remember, such gifts are no measure of true love. The sugar in the spell represents exotic spices from faraway lands; the pearls, treasures from deep and secret places.

You will need

A golden candle (the color must be true gold, rather than yellow); benzoin oil; some sugar; a string of pearls

★ ON A THURSDAY NIGHT NEAR TO A FULL MOON, ROLL THE CANDLE IN BENZOIN OIL AND THEN IN SUGAR. Allow the sugar to dry hard on the candle, then place it in your special holder. Wind the string of pearls around the bottom of the candle holder, then light the candle. As it begins to burn, say: *"I am precious, / My love too; / What real value, / Have I for you?"* Sit well back as the candle burns, as it might spit a little with the burning sugar. Keep a close eye on the candle while it burns down, repeating the words at regular intervals. ★ THIS SPELL SHOULD BRING INTERESTING RESULTS. While it may not provide you with a millionaire, you may find that your previously undemonstrative lover starts to bring you little gifts.

An extraordinarily literal result of this spell for my girlfriend Lucy was a regular invitation to vacation in the West Indies, where coincidentally (or not!) sugar is produced.

Walk on gold ★ A money talisman to be in the habit of using. Certain lucky charms seem
to have a proven effect in bringing many small parcels of prosperity continually over time. In many respects this is greatly to be preferred to a larger sum that is here today and gone all too soon. Try either or both of the following spells if you would like to be a person whose luck with money and business success just keeps ticking over nicely.

You will need
A "gold" coin (gold colored will do); a pad of absorbent cotton, if needed

★ This practice was long regarded by wise women as the best way of ensuring that there is always money in an emergency. It became so settled in the imagination that, ultimately, it found its way into wedding ceremonies in the rhyme *"Something old, / Something new, / Something borrowed, / Something blue. / And a silver sixpence in your shoe."* The original practice was to put a piece of gold in your shoe, first showing it to the sun and asking his blessing that your fortunes would, from that day forward, be surrounded by a glow of golden brightness. In this spell, as you do so you should say the words *"I need no jewels nor bags of gold; / But may my purse have enough to hold."* ★ If the coin feels uncomfortable, cover it with a cotton pad and secure it where it will not cause a blister. Place your lucky coin in your shoe as often as possible, and be careful never to spend it.

Silvery moon ★ For this money charm you need to order a special piece of silver,
which symbolizes the fruits of success. This should be a personal choice. Good examples of appropriate symbols would be any nut or fruit (to symbolize the harvest), an ear of corn, or a peony flower.

You will need
A piece of personally commissioned silver to charge with the moon's rays

★ Keep your piece of silver in a small pouch until the night you charge it with the moon's light, which should be on one of the following dates: Lammas (August 1), Beltane (May 1), Rowan Day (May 13), Midsummer Day (June 21), or St. Swithin's Day (July 15). Place the silver on your forehead, then hold it up to the moon and draw the tide of her magnetic power into the metal, saying: *"May my fortunes grow from this day."* Wear the charm somewhere close to you, but not in public view (even on a key chain is fine). Touch the talisman and look to the moon whenever you need special help.

To climb the corporate ladder ★ A SPELL SPECIALLY FORMULATED

FOR SWIFT PROGRESS AT WORK. This spell has two real applications. If you are just starting a new job, you should perform this ceremony on the first day, when you return from work. Alternatively, it would be appropriate to use this spell if you are opening a small business, such as a shop, in a field in which there are many other competitors.

YOU WILL NEED

An acorn; a jade plant, planted in a green pot; a small stepladder

★ WHEN YOU COLLECT YOUR ACORN, TOUCH THE OAK TREE AND ASK FOR ITS BLESSING, AND POUR A SMALL CUP OF ALE OR WINE AROUND ITS ROOTS. Having done this before you start the job, take the acorn with you in your pocket for the whole of the first day, and touch it each time you are introduced to someone new or go into a new room or work area. At the end of the working day, go back to your home and place the jade plant at your front door. Push the acorn into the soil around the jade plant and say: *"My talents all shall blossom forth, / My skills be in demand; / And from this day promotion shall, / With luck, go hand in hand."* Place the little plant at the front door on a small stepladder, which makes an unusual plant holder. If you like, arrange other plants on the lower steps, but the jade plant must go at the top. ★ IF YOU LIVE IN A WARM ENOUGH CLIMATE FOR THE JADE PLANT TO LIVE OUTSIDE, forgo the ladder and plant it on high ground or place it on a top step. Keep the plant healthy and well, and you will meet with much success in your chosen career. If you have a front and a back door, work the spell with two plants and two acorns, placing one plant at either door.

GOOD LUCK & BEST WISHES

The oak bath ★ A SPELL TO ATTRACT GOOD LUCK AND CLEANSE THE SPIRIT. There is no reason

why one person should seem to land on their feet all the time while another, with just as much hard work and good intention, seems constantly to be missing out in life. If you want to ensure that luck and good fortune are never far from you, soak away the stresses of life in this rather unusual bath.

YOU WILL NEED

A handful of clean oak leaves; a few drops of lemongrass oil; an acorn; a length of red cord

★ ON THE NEW MOON, FILL A BATHTUB WITH HOT WATER AND PLACE A HANDFUL OF NICELY CLEANED OAK LEAVES AND THE OIL INTO IT. Before you get into the bath, hold the acorn and say these words: *"Cleanse my spirit, cleanse my soul, / Enrich my life with a happiness whole"* and look at the acorn on the palm of your hand. Charge the acorn with your mind, and instruct it to be the talisman of your joys—ask that it govern the tides of your life and change it in a positive way. Lay the acorn on the edge of the bath, climb in, and relax, breathing in the smell and the spirit of the ancient oak trees—strong, secure, beautiful. After your bath, sleep with the acorn under your pillow. ★ THE FOLLOWING DAY, TAKE THE ACORN AS EARLY AS POSSIBLE INTO THE RAYS OF THE MORNING SUN, THEN WRAP THE RED CORD AROUND YOUR INDEX FINGER. Concentrate all your strength onto the acorn, and touch your beribboned finger to your "third eye" (between your eyebrows). See your new life dawning without any negativity or unhappiness. Wish good on yourself, your family, your friends, and your neighbors. Now pop the acorn into your pocket and carry it around for the day to charge it with your personality. Whenever you think of it, smile to yourself about the acorn, the symbol of a new optimism in your life. ★ THE ACORN IS NOW YOUR PROTECTIVE TALISMAN, AND AT EVERY NEW MOON YOU MUST WISH GENTLY ON IT FOR A POSITIVE, LUCKIER LIFE.

Golden radiance ★ TO ATTRACT POWERFUL LIGHT INTO YOUR HOME.

YOU WILL NEED

A gold-colored cord or piece of rope; bunches of sunflowers; a golden dinner candle; a small pouch or coin purse

★ EVERY DAY FOR A WEEK, AT SUNSET, CLEANSE YOUR HOUSE BY WALKING THROUGH EACH ROOM TRAILING THE GOLD CORD BEHIND YOU. This done, place a bunch of sunflowers in each room (where they will remain for a week after the first night). Then, on your altar, dining table, or hearth, burn a golden candle, notched equally in seven places to burn down one mark every night. While the candle burns, allow yourself to laugh inwardly, and focus positively on attracting happiness and luck (not necessarily of the material kind); draw the optimism of a sunny day right into your house. ★ AT THE END OF THE WEEK, TIE THE CORD IN A BOW AROUND THE CANDLE STUMP AND PLACE IT IN A POUCH OR COIN PURSE TO BE CARRIED IN YOUR HANDBAG, IN YOUR BRIEFCASE, OR EVEN IN YOUR CAR. This spell is best performed in the month of Leo, late-July–August, when the sun's strength is at its zenith. (If you should be in the Southern Hemisphere, reverse this advice and do it in the month of Aquarius, late-January–February.)

A woven talisman ★ FOR LUCK THROUGHOUT THE YEAR.

YOU WILL NEED

Some burlap or coarse linen to make a pouch; colored threads; betony; 3 ribbons, each 12 inches long
(1 your representative color [see pages 151–152], 1 white, and 1 violet); a sprig of birch or rowan

★ ON A SUNDAY OR A THURSDAY, SEW TOGETHER A SMALL POUCH FROM THE FABRIC AND EMBROIDER IT WITH THE COLORED THREADS TO MAKE AN EMBLEM FOR HAPPINESS AND LUCK (SEE PAGES 154–157). Fill the pouch three-quarters full with betony (dried or fresh), a powerful talisman against evil. Now weave the three ribbons around the birch or rowan sprig quite tightly, making a kind of attractive braid. As you weave, feel your luck changing and see yourself and your family enjoying the fruits of good works. Place the finished talisman to your "third eye" (between your eyebrows) and wish for peace, health, and happiness; then tuck the sprig into the pouch and sew it up. Touch it first to your heart, next to your hands, and lastly to your brow. ★ PUT YOUR LUCKY CHARM SOMEWHERE SAFE, AND TAKE IT WITH YOU EACH TIME YOU NEED A LITTLE LUCK.

The sweet pea spell ★ BEANS AND PEAS HAVE LONG BEEN ASSOCIATED WITH THE

GODDESS MOTHER EARTH. Beans, in particular, have a wonderful perfume and represent nature's exotic harvest. The sweet pea, a purely ornamental version and highly fragranced, is a special link between our earth and the spirit/fairy world. Try this spell for luck, which will come to you within two weeks of the appearance of the first bloom.

YOU WILL NEED

A pack of sweet pea seeds (any colors); an ornamental hair clasp

★ PLANT A CROP OF SWEET PEAS IN A SPECIAL PLACE. THIS CAN BE IN TUBS OR WINDOW BOXES OR IN THE GROUND; BUT, WHATEVER THE LOCATION, IT SHOULD BE KEPT JUST FOR THE SWEET PEAS. (They do best where summers are cool; alternatively, they can be grown in a greenhouse.) As you sow each seed, dedicate it to the goddess (call her by whatever name you will). Tend your seeds lovingly and water carefully, saying a prayer over them each day until they flower. On the first evening that they have bloomed, inhale their perfume deep into your soul, drinking the fragrance right down to your feet, and thank Mother Nature for her bounty — such beauty and joy from something so tiny. Ask that your life may be like this, with many sweet and lovely things arising from small, happy deeds. Request that good luck come to you or even that a particular wish comes true. Now, cut a perfect flower and place it on an altar to the goddess, in your home. ★ EACH DAY, REPLACE THE FLOWER WITH ANOTHER PERFECT FRESH BLOOM, WEARING YESTERDAY'S IN YOUR HAIR OR BUTTONHOLE. After one week, gather the flowers into a posy, place it on the altar, and secure it with a hair clasp, telling the goddess it is for her hair. Within one more week, your luck will alter in a positive way or your wish will be granted.

The hazel chaplet ★ A TALISMAN FOR LUCK ON SPECIAL OCCASIONS. On Beltane (May 1)

or Midsummer Day (June 21), braid some slender hazel branches into a chaplet, or wreath, for your head. Decorate the headpiece with flowers and wear it throughout the day for luck. A man could weave the hazel into a brooch to wear on his coat instead. At sundown, make a special wish for something very precious, not frivolous, and place the chaplet next to your bed. ★ WITHIN THE NEXT 12 MONTHS, YOU WILL HAVE YOUR ANSWER.

Apple-watered rowan ★ A SPELL TO BRING PROSPERITY AND YOUTHFULNESS TO

THE DWELLERS OF YOUR HOME. The apple is sacred to the goddess, perhaps because it has a star within if you cut the fruit clean across. ★ PLANT A BABY ROWAN, OR MOUNTAIN ASH, TREE TO THE EAST OF YOUR HOUSE or in a large pot in good light, facing east for the morning sun, and water it every day with a tiny amount of applejack (a rough hard cider). Tell the spirits you are giving them a special libation, and ask in return that they spiritually water your family with a libation of health and prosperity. Nurture your tree, and the gods will honor you in turn.

My neighbor and good friend, Sally, performed this spell using apples from one of her many beautiful Somerset apple trees and made the unselfish wish for a more beautiful and natural garden. She is not so sure about the results; her garden is certainly very beautiful, and full of wonderful birds, but it has also attracted badgers, who now come nightly to eat the windfall from her trees. Her friends and neighbors love to watch these delightful creatures, but they are causing some havoc in the rest of her garden.

The rosemary blessing ★ To ensure success in a venture, or to bless a house or journey.

You will need

A few sprigs of rosemary; green or gold ribbons; a glass of wine

★ Make a rosemary charm on All Hallows' Day (November 1) or Beltane (May 1) by making a crude doll from a few sprigs of the herb tied with green or gold ribbons into arms and legs on a body. Place it in your kitchen. Take a leftover sprig of rosemary from your workings and, on the eve of your departure or move to a new home or the project you wish to bless, pop it into a glass of wine and drink a toast to good spirits and positive luck. ★ Share this toast with anyone else involved in the project for which you seek luck.

An ancient exorcism ★ To rid the house of bad spirits. This routine is as ancient as the hills and employs the favorite tool of all witches, the broom. Use this if you really feel you have a negative "spirit" abiding with you. On the full moon, sweep with the broom across the threshold of your home and then bang it three times on the step. Continue through every room in the house with the broom, sweeping up a veritable storm of energy. Now sweep backward through the house to the front or back door and symbolically chase out the last of the bad energy. Bang the broom thrice again, and replace the broom behind the door. Light a candle in the main room of the house, in front of a mirror, and direct all evil to leave. Let the candle burn right down, then offer a blessing to the spirit to return to its proper plane of consciousness.

To spread love and good feeling ★ THIS SPELL IS ONE OF SPIRITUAL

GENEROSITY and can be carried out as a peace offering to the community, on a vigil of any kind, or even when a group of people you know have been having a difficult time. It is akin to a prayer for the nation.

YOU WILL NEED

3 candles: 1 pink, 1 yellow, and 1 white; paper and pen; a vase of pinks

★ LIGHT THE THREE CANDLES AT ANY HOUR OF ANY DAY. Write down the names of the people (or family or school or even country) you wish to help, and place the paper, like a petition, in front of the candle. Place a vase of pinks (preferably fragrant) on the table, and, with one or two friends, link hands and focus energy to send from the candles to the people in need. After some minutes start to imagine the people flying, soaring above the grayness of their woes. Ring them with light in your mind, and picture them victorious over misery and depression. Now bring them gently back to earth and imagine presenting them with a flower. Extinguish the candles and, if possible, take one of the pinks to the person or family or group in need; better still, give each person a flower. Repeat the process another night, as a booster, and very soon they will appear much less despondent and more confident.

★ THIS SPELL ALSO WORKS IF YOU HAVE FRIENDS WHO HAVE BEEN FEUDING; it might help get them talking to each other again.

The protection amulet ★ TO DRIVE AWAY BAD LUCK OR SOMEONE'S ENMITY. If you

believe you are the victim of some unhappy person's malevolent thoughts toward you, this ritual should neutralize their negativity.

YOU WILL NEED

A whole head of garlic; yarrow; 2 homemade pouches; white ribbon

★ FOR ONE WEEK, PLACE A WHOLE HEAD OF GARLIC ABOVE YOUR FRONT DOOR, INSTRUCTING IT EACH NIGHT BY MOONLIGHT TO SOAK UP ANY POISON AIMED AT YOU. One week to the day, bury the garlic in the garden, saying: *"Hollow thoughts and evil sorts remain in darkness ever; / Preserve my wit, that I submit to ill-thought wishes never."* Now tie some yarrow into two homemade pouches and secure them with white ribbon. Place one at the front door and another within the house near the main living area, behind or just above a mirror. ★ THIS WILL DEFLECT ANY UNCHARITABLE WISHES AWAY FROM YOU AND BACK TO THE PERSON WHO IS SENDING THEM.

The rainbow spell for happiness and joy ★ This is

THE BEST SPELL OF ALL TO DO, FOR IT COVERS EVERYTHING IN THE BOOK IN ONE WAY OR ANOTHER. It asks for nothing specific and everything in general—somewhat like those children's fairy tales where the good fairy used to grant the lucky hero three wishes, and if the hero was wise enough he asked for "health, wealth, and happiness." Try this if you have no specific requests but would like to try a magic spell to see if it changes your life in any way.

You will need

7 candles, 7 ribbons, and 7 flowers, one each of each color of the rainbow

The rainbow colors also represent the old planets of the Zodiac: red for Mars, orange for Sun, yellow for Moon, green for Mercury, blue for Venus, indigo for Jupiter, and violet for Saturn. ★ TIE EACH CANDLE AT THE BASE WITH ITS MATCHING RIBBON. In each of seven rooms in your house, or in seven places in one room if you live somewhere smaller, place one candle with its matching flower in a stem vase to make a simple yet colorful altar. Open all the windows and ask for nature's blessings. Promise to honor nature more attentively in the future, by leaving out crumbs for the birds, growing more plants and flowers, not killing creatures who come inside, and recycling as much as you can for the sake of the environment. Promise, too, to try to smile more and not to criticize others too much. ★ LIGHT YOUR CANDLES IN THE ORDER OF THE RAINBOW COLORS (AS ABOVE) AND FEEL THE COLOR OF EACH LIGHT BURNING INTO YOU. Sit in the middle of the room (or house) and surround yourself mentally with the swirling light of every color. After one hour, extinguish the candles and untie the ribbons, then wind them loosely together into a braid. Repeat this procedure for six more nights, undoing the ribbons from the braid and retying them each time. At the end of the week, when the flowers will have wilted and the candles burned down, take the ribbons and weave them into a neat braid. ★ THIS WILL BECOME YOUR MOST POWERFUL TALISMAN AND WILL ALWAYS ATTRACT RAINBOW COLORS INTO YOUR LIFE. Recharge the braid at an open window on one day of every month, and always keep it in a special place.

The tree/moon calendar of the Druids ★ The months

OF THE YEAR WERE MARKED OUT BY THE CELTS IN THE THIRTEEN MOONS, which they named after the sacred trees. Each moon was measured from full, that being its time of greatest power, to full; and the first moon of the year was that falling closest to Yule, December 21. These months also have connotations that might help your magic. ★ IN ORDER, THE MOON MONTHS ARE: Birch or, less usually, olive: the moon of beginning; rowan: the travel moon; ash: the healing moon, ruling tides; alder: the spirit moon, concerned with self-guidance; willow: the moon of love and fertility, the real witch's moon; hawthorn: the peace moon; oak (approximately midyear): the strongest moon; holly: the moon to disenchant, moon of prophecy; hazel: the wise moon, moon of actuality; vine: the moon of the harvest; ivy: the moon of protection and partnership; reed: the domestic moon, moon of motherhood; elder (sometimes myrtle): the moon of completion, moon of banishment. ★ SOME MAGIC WAS WORKED OVER THE COURSE OF THE WHOLE YEAR, BETWEEN THE MOONS OF THE BIRCH AND ELDER TREES. You may wish to enhance your magic by incorporating a branch or some wood from the relevant tree in your spell, according to the time when you are performing it.

A note on petitioning the gods ★ All systems of ancient magic

WORKED WITH THE POWER AND BLESSING OF THE GODS. In this book the religious element is left to choice, and it is written so that it can dovetail with any personal religious beliefs. However, if you feel it helps to relate your spell-working back to the magic of the ancients, here follows a short list of the most commonly petitioned gods and goddesses and the matters that fall within their domains. In each case, the god or goddess is given his or her Greek name followed by the Roman name. ★ IN MATTERS OF LOVE: *Aphrodite/Venus*. For divination and prophecy: *Apollo*. In matters concerning our deep emotions and our secret selves: *Selene/Luna*. Concerning maternity and childbirth: *Hera/Juno*. In matters of luck and fate: *Zeus/Jupiter*. For protection: *Hermes/Mercury*. Concerning healing: *Asclepius and Hygieia*

Essential oils in magic ★

IN MY GRANDMOTHER'S DAY, many of the fragrant brews she used in spell-making were unsightly, to say the least. The properties of the herbs and their essences, however, were crucial to the psychological state of the spell-maker, and unpleasant colors sometimes had to be endured. Not so today, when aromatherapy has made little bottles of essential oils familiar to all. The short list here is only a selection of the oils most often used or those that have a multiplicity of functions. Use them according to instruction for room fragrancing, candle anointing, and bathing.

BASIL: a good all-round oil, focuses the mind and cheers the spirits.

BERGAMOT: helps combat introversion and downward mood spirals.

CAMOMILE: excellent when you're worried or tired.

CAMPHOR: a good telepathy oil; disenchants unwanted admirers.

CLARY SAGE: restarts your flat battery.

CYPRESS: sometimes used to calm anxiety and jealousy.

EUCALYPTUS: cuts through the ether; a good clairvoyant oil.

FENNEL: curbs appetite.

FRANKINCENSE: a prince of oils, excellent for leveling emotions and allaying fears.

GRAPEFRUIT: traditional for detaching someone from the past.

HYSSOP: mainly for money and prosperity.

JASMINE: very sensual, but expensive; a lover's scent; helps to overcome sexual apprehension.

JUNIPER: often used in protection rites and general love spells.

LAVENDER: useful for everything: passion, purification, insecurity, protection. Also invaluable in the first aid box for treating burns, bites, and skin complaints.

LEMON: deals with selfish thoughts.

LEMON VERBENA: traditional scent for love messages.

LEMONGRASS: stimulates the system; good for someone who shows lack of interest in love.

LETTUCE: sleep inducing, calms overly strong sexual appetite.

MANDRAKE: for use on altars only. As famous as Macbeth, the strongest magic herb.

MARIGOLD: telepathic; nurtures love.

MARJORAM: calms hostility and anxiety, ideal for reunion dinners.

MEADOWSWEET: may not be available as an oil, but strew the herb on altars. Very cheering.

MELISSA (LEMON BALM): a female herb; also good for treating fright and shock.

MYRRH: for talking to the divinity.

NEROLI AND ORANGE: a marriage oil.

ORRIS: if unavailable as oil, use powdered root. Good for all love matters.

PATCHOULI: brightens the mind; improves creative energies.

PEONY: (perfume oil) very exotic; also good for money spells.

PEPPERMINT: the right oil to use for studying and focusing thoughts.

ROSE GERANIUM: like lavender —a thousand purposes! Erotic; creates and breaks attachments, and thus is useful in many spells.

ROSE ATTAR: pure rose oil: the most valuable oil in love spells. Soothes nerves and counteracts sadness or grief. Can level thoughts that are too strongly nostalgic.

ROSEMARY: a male scent. For clarity of mind, and bringing about action.

SANDALWOOD: a good love oil: deals with feelings of self-doubt, and lingers in the imagination; also very purifying.

VANILLA: exotic. Used in love charms and potpourris.

TEA TREE: the Australian answer to lavender; sets healing in process.

VIOLET: wash hands and bathe head with this or rose (diluted in warm water) before performing love spells for a really powerful current in your magic.

YLANG-YLANG: the third crucial sensual oil; counteracts anger and frustration.

Colors in magic ★ Some spells call for the use of a candle or color of your own

CHOICE; indeed, colors will come into your magic regularly, and you may decide to incorporate a special color of your own to give each spell a stronger personal connection to you.

★ COLOR BY NUMBER

I am a great believer in the use of numbers for luck and symbolic power. We all have a number, which can be deduced by adding together the digits of the day (forget month and year) that you are born on. If you were born on the 17th, add together 1 and 7 to make 8, the number that influences you every day. This works well for magic. If you were born on the 11th, the 22nd, or the 29th, do not reduce these beyond 11 and 22—these are master numbers with their own specific color. Work out your number and check the spectrum below.

1 (including 10): flame red or apricot; 2: white or salmon pink; 3: ruby red or rose; 4: green or indigo; 5: cherry pink or wisteria; 6: mustard or heliotrope; 7: magenta, brick, or purple; 8: canary yellow, buff, or ivory; 9: lavender, olive, or straw; 11: silver; 22: gold.

★ COLOR BY SIGN

If astrology is a more familiar tool for you, take your color choice from your sun sign. This list is taken from the old associations, thought to be Egyptian in origin:

Aries: bright red; Taurus: dark yellow; Gemini: violet; Cancer: sea green or silver; Leo: orange or golden yellow; Virgo: indigo; Libra: light yellow; Scorpio: very dark red or black; Sagittarius: lilac-purple; Capricorn: dark blue; Aquarius: light blue or dazzling white; Pisces: iridescent purple.

★ A NOTE ON ANOINTING CANDLES

Many spells call for an "anointed" candle. This simple procedure is best achieved by dabbing the designated oil onto the wick, thence along the candle itself, and leaving it to penetrate for a few minutes. If you prefer, put a few drops of oil into some spring water, pour it into a small perfume atomizer, and spray the scent along the candle, especially near the top.

Lucky symbols ★ FOR MAGIC TO WORK PROPERLY, IT MUST CONTAIN AN ELEMENT OF

INDIVIDUALISM, FOR IT IS A PIECE OF YOURSELF, YOUR OWN PSYCHE OR SOUL, THAT YOU ARE GIVING TO THE WORKING. The best way to do this is to add one symbolic charm, or perhaps just a plain object that you identify with yourself, and/or with the person you love for spells involving them. This might range from a straightforward representation, such as a rebus (picture-word) revolving around your or your beloved's name (an arrow, say, for a "Fletcher," a piece of metal for a "Smith," etc.), an object you and/or your partner love (a musical note for a musician or music lover, a boat for a traveler or sailing enthusiast), or, best of all, a more mystical symbol which you alone understand. The following is a selection of symbols that have a long association with magic ritual. Choose freely.

ACORN: symbol of the sacred oak and of growth from small beginnings; also fertility and divine protection.

ANGELS AND CHERUBS, OR PUTTI: messengers of the gods and, in antiquity, harbingers of love.

APPLE: sacred to Venus / Aphrodite; the fruit has a star when cut across the middle. A golden apple signifies persistence.

ARROW: attribute of Cupid: in gold it kindles love, but in baser metal it spurns love.

BASKET: of flowers, signifies hope; of fruit, fertility and passion.

BAT: symbol of the passing night and the witching hour.

BEE: strongly connected with Venus; signifies hard work; also humility in love, and the healing of hurt, recalling Cupid being stung by a bee while stealing a honeycomb. A beehive is a blessing of love on your home, a place where sweet honey will grow. A very lucky charm.

BELL: to claim somebody's attention.

BIRD: symbolic of the soul. A goldfinch is said to have acquired its red spot swooping to pluck a thorn from Christ's brow on his path to Calvary; an owl is wise; a British blackbird is especially magical, as its song enchants the listener; a dove is the bird of Venus and is a well-known symbol of peace.

BOAR: signifies passion untamed.

BOAT: someone who travels or is abroad.

BOOK: symbolic of someone learned; also knowledge itself.

BOW: a hunter; or the same attributes as Cupid's arrow.

BUTTERFLY: reincarnation and, specific to love, gentleness.

CAMEL: ability to endure time apart from a loved one.

CANDLE: many symbolic references to light and knowledge; in love, the kindling of the spark into a steady flame.

CARDS: according to individual divination. The ace of hearts: an invitation to love; the nine of hearts: a wish fulfilled; a king or queen: the loved one; a knave: someone not to be trusted.

CARNATION, OR PINK: a symbol of betrothal, especially if red.

CAT: lucky for witches; they know the secrets of the night.

CHERRY: the fruit of paradise.

CLOVER: always lucky, as cattle fed on it were seen to thrive; a four-leaf clover is especially lucky.

CRUCIBLE: symbol of alchemy.

DICE: a gamble.

DOLPHIN: these creatures drew the chariot of Venus, hence they bring love.

DRAGON, DRAGONFLY: fertility and power; also the symbol of anything Welsh!

FATHER TIME: he unveils truth and shows that, in the end, right must prevail.

FLOWERS: from Flora, the bringer of spring, thus hope and renewal.

FOUNTAIN: Representative of the garden of love.

FROG: privy to the secrets of witchcraft, a lucky emblem.

GLOBE: someone who has lived in more than one country; or, the desire to travel.

GRASSHOPPER: herald of good news.

HARE: sometimes a witch, a messenger, or possibly a timid person.

HONEY: in a pot, or as a comb, symbol of strength and sweetness in love.

HORN: powerful talisman against deceit.

IVY: immortality, as an evergreen, thus tenacity in love and all ventures.

KEY: fidelity in love.

KNOT: symbol of an indissoluble union. The strongest is in a figure eight.

LADDER: ascent, or upward progress.

LADYBUG: very lucky symbol of providence in the home, and a good omen for travel.

LAUREL: in a wreath, the prize of knowledge; also, excellence.

LILY: purity and devotion; a tiger lily is passionate love.

LOOM: symbol of the woman weaving, and so, enchanting.

LYRE: suggestive of poetry and the ability to woo. Where Orpheus laid his lyre, violets arose.

MIRROR: self-knowledge and truth.

MOON: lamp of the night. Central to most magic-working and love divination; connected with the ebb and flow of emotions.

MOUNTAIN: something of enormous size or foreign.

MUSICAL INSTRUMENTS: symbols of love, as musicians were regarded as the children of Venus.

MYRTLE: powerful talisman for fidelity in marriage.

OAK: the tree of strength and wisdom, most sacred to the Druids. Love will conquer.

PANSY, OR HEARTSEASE: the most potent flower for love.

PESTLE AND MORTAR: the magician or alchemist.

POPPY: symbol of hypnotic power, sleep, and dreams.

PRIMROSE: excellent talisman for youth and fertility.

QUINCE: from Venus, a powerful fertility fruit and symbol of marriage.

RABBIT: strongly connected with Venus, and of course, fecundity.

RAINBOW: arc of communication with the gods, personified by Iris in classical mythology. Very strong in magic, since the blending of all the colors makes the perfect white. Recreating the rainbow spectrum around your dwelling ensures good fortune.

RIBBON: see Thread.

RING: Universal symbol of eternal love and authority.

ROSE: flower of the Virgin. Especially, the bloom of love, since it is sacred to Venus; legend tells that at her birth, roses suddenly appeared. The pricks from its thorns are likened to the wounds of love. Originally the white rose was sacred to lovers, but when Venus hastened to help the dying Adonis, a thorn pricked her foot and stained the rose red with her blood. Thus, the red rose became a symbol of passion.

SAIL: also sacred to Venus, signifying her birth. Used often to symbolize a traveler.

SEA HORSE: extremely fortunate symbol; the messenger adapted for sea and land, beloved of the gods.

SHELL: especially scallop or nautilus. Symbol of foreigners. Especially strong in love, as it was made sacred in the birth of Venus. Also powerful for blessings of the home, since it is itself a home to sea creatures.

SNAIL: epitomizes patience, a virtue in witchcraft. An excellent general charm.

STAG: usually a personal emblem. Known for fleetness and sharp senses, which help it to avoid capture. It is connected with the sense of hearing, and its stillness is aspired to by practitioners of magic.

STARS: literally, divinities; to speak to a star is to converse with the gods themselves.

STORK: the bringer of news, connected with Mercury.

SUNFLOWER AND, SOMETIMES, MARIGOLD: flower of ardent love, turned forever to the sun. Used in magic to disperse gloom.

SWAN: sacred to Venus, and thus lovers, because swans drew her sea chariot.

SWORD: emblem of justice. Sometimes, in love, it represents a tortured soul.

THIMBLE: powerful charm, symbol of patient work. Can also signify anyone who works with his or her hands.

THREAD: usually woven into three, symbolizing the Three Fates. In magic this transmutes to a ribbon.

TRIDENT: emblem of the sea and of Neptune. Sometimes chosen by a Piscean as his or her personal charm.

UNICORN: most magical of all animals, and protector of women. Allays poison. People who see unicorns can see fairies.

VINE: the harvest, most significant part of the calendar in magic.

VIOLET: humility and sweetness. A necklace of violets protects against deception, and it is sometimes regarded as the flower of Cupid. Violets sprang up to feed Io when she was changed into a heifer by Jupiter to protect her from Juno's jealousy. Thus, they are the food of love.

VIOLIN OR VIOLA: specific to the "music of the spheres," and thus beguiling love.

WAND: symbol of knowledge and directed thought. The talisman of the magician.

WEB: symbol of spinning and spiders, and thought to be very lucky. Spiders often help humans who have shown warmth and

regard for living creatures. The web is connected with the "web of life" and the strands of human destiny.

WHEAT OR CORN: fertility. Also a sign of some special news.

WIND: either Zephyr, the warm west wind, which, as husband of Flora, brings the flowers of spring; or Boreas, the cold wind from the north, which terminates affairs of the heart or signifies a long period of endurance.

WINGS: Victory of the spirit.

YARROW: the witch's herb and, formally, a posy for a new bride.

Index

Also by Titania Hardie
SPELLCARDS Health and Happiness
SPELLCARDS Love and Success
TITANIA'S FORTUNE CARDS
WITCH IN THE KITCHEN
LOVE ELIXIRS
Published by Cedco

PUBLISHING DIRECTOR Anne Furniss

DESIGN Johnson Banks

LAYOUT Jim Smith

PRODUCTION Nancy Roberts

Published by Cedco Publishing in 2001
100 Pelican Way, San Rafael, CA 94901
www.cedco.com

First published in 2001 by Quadrille Publishing Limited,
Alhambra House, 27-31 Charing Cross Road, London WC2H OLS

ISBN 0-7683-2499-8

Printed and bound in Germany